DEVELOPMENT PLANNING FOR MINORITIES

A Study

R.S. Tiwari

ANMOL PUBLICATIONS PVT. LTD.
NEW DELHI - 110 002 (INDIA)

ANMOL PUBLICATIONS PVT. LTD.
H.O.: 4374/4B, Ansari Road, Darya Ganj,
New Delhi-110 002 (India)
Ph.: 23278000, 23261597
B.O.: No. 1015, Ist Main Road, BSK IIIrd Stage
IIIrd Phase, IIIrd Block,
Bangalore - 560 085 (India)
Visit us at: www.anmolpublications.com

Development Planning for Minorities

First Published, 2006

ISBN 81-261-2927-1

[This book is published with partial publication grant from GIDS, Lucknow. However, the responsibility for the facts stated, opinions expressed and conclusion reached is solely that of the Author and not of the Institute.]

PRINTED IN INDIA

Printed at Mehra Offset Press, Delhi.

Contents

Contents

Preface

It has increasingly been recognized that a majority of minority population is engaged in traditional activities, such as, handloom, powerloom, textile printing and other handicrafts, like, embroidery, chikan, zari, etc. Also, they are engaged in wood carving, metal work, carpet weaving, perfumery, leather work, besides in transport, manufacturing and trading. Remaining depends on salaried jobs in the government, public and private organizations or self-employed in service sector. Those residing in rural hinterland are engaged as labour, small and marginal farmers, artisans or self-employed in small scale trade. It has been experienced that working hours in these employments are very long and strenuous, while earnings are meagre. As a result, their living conditions are dismal resulting into poverty, educational backwardness and poor health conditions.

Various poverty alleviation programmes, i.e. Integrated Rural Development Programme (IRDP), Drought Prone Area Programme (DPAP) and the Jawahar Rozgar Yojana (JRY) have been in operation in the State for quite some time. Besides, Training of Rural Youth for Self-Employment Programme (TRYSEM), Total Literacy Campaign (TLC), Immunization Campaign, Nehru Yuva Kendras, Minority Finance and Development Corporation (MFDC) have also existed. Several NGOs are also engaged to tackle the problems posed by poverty and unemployment. However, benefits from socio-economic development programmes have not percolated from privileged top to deprived downtrodden sections of society.

This has been recognized on account of inbuilt structural problems in the existing Indian economic system. It is recognized that problems of poverty and unemployment needs to be handled from 'population end' by pursuing 'area based approach' rather than that of 'programme based approach.' Present study considering minority households in selected villages, blocks and cities in Rampur district is a modest attempt in this direction. In particular, study examines empirically: (i) social characteristics of minorities, (ii) economic characteristics of minorities, (iii) housing characteristics and health conditions of minorities, (iv) employment structure, welfare programmes and development of minorities, and (v) policy recommendations based on the general findings of the study. The indepth socio-economic understanding about minority households has been considered as an appropriate basis for policy recommendations to improve the socio-economic conditions. Thus, 'area based approach' rather than 'programme based approach' has been followed in the present study for solving the socio-economic problems of minorities.

Present study received invaluable help and cooperation from many distinguished persons and intellectuals from its inception to its present form. Mr. Siraj Hussain, IAS, Secretary, Minorities Welfare and Muslim Waqf, Government of Uttar Pradesh, has been the main source of guidance and encouragement. The fruitful discussions held with him in various meetings gave intellectual inputs and guidance at various stages of the study. Besides, his predecessor, Mr. Mohd. Haleem Khan, IAS, has been the main source of initiation of the preset study. I am extremely thankful to them for their invaluable support. Dr. Sultan Ahmad, Deputy Director, Directorate of Minority Welfare, Lucknow and Mr. Riyasat Hussain, District Minority Welfare Officer, Rampur helped in furnishing the relevant information required for the study. I express my thank to them for their invaluable support.

Prof. M.S. Ashraf, my senior colleague, Giri Institute of Development Studies, Lucknow extended invaluable intellectual support and cooperation since inception to its present form. I feel extremely thankful to him for his kind cooperation and support.

I received constructive support from research team consisting of Dr. Lallan Dubey, Shri R.K. Jaiswal, Shri K.S. Negi, Shri Mohd. Akmal Kidwai, Ms. Khalda Bano, Shri Leela Nath Mishra and Shri Mohd. Kaleem. All of them helped whole heartedly. I am thankful to all of them.

Various minority households, units and establishments of Rampur also gave unhesitantly full cooperation to our research team in collecting the relevant information. I thank all these individuals and organizations.

I also owe my indebtedness to the Minorities Welfare and Muslim Waqf, Government of Uttar Pradesh for extending generous financial support for carrying out the present study.

I would also like to extend my thankfulness to Prof. G.P. Mishra, former Director and Prof. A.K. Singh, present Director, Giri Institute of Development Studies, Lucknow for extending invaluable intellectual and efficient administrative support from its inception to its present form.

I am also thankful to the Library staff for extending the required facility and to Mr. Manoharan K. for word processing the report timely and efficiently.

Needless to mention, the present study is the outcome of goodwill, support and suggestions I enjoyed from all these sources. I am, however, alone responsible for all the errors and omission remained in the present study.

-- R.S. Tiwari

Giri Institute of Development Studies
Lucknow 226024

1

Introduction: Framework of the Study

Background

Muslims constitute a significant proportion of the population in the state of Uttar Pradesh. According to 1991 Census, Muslim population was 17.30 per cent of total population in the state. Nearly one-fourth (23.73 per cent), of total Muslims in India, live in Uttar Pradesh. Also, as per Census 1981, larger percentage of Muslim population (32.10 per cent) than the general population (19.00 per cent) lived in the urban areas.

A majority of the urban minority population is engaged in traditional industries, such as, handloom, powerloom, block making, wood carving, metal work, carpet weaving, perfumery, leather work, glass work, textile printing and other handicrafts, such as, embroidery, chikan, zari, etc. Many of them are also engaged in transport, manufacturing and exports. The remaining depends on salaried jobs in the government, public and private organizations or in self-employed service sector. Those residing in the rural areas are engaged as labour, small and marginal farmers, artisans or self-employed in small scale trade.

The problems of illiteracy and educational backwardness, unemployment and poverty, high infant mortality and morbidity rates, poor living conditions and unsanitary environment are gigantic for all sections of population. Such conditions are, however, more intense among the minority population. They have suffered more primarily due to lack of education conditioned by their poor economic conditions. A majority of the minority earners belong to the categories of artisans, skilled workers, small and marginal farmers and self-employed in the service sector where most of the household members contribute to the economic activity. Their working hours are very long and strenuous, while their earnings are meagre. They have, generally, no time to spare for education for their children as they are also engaged in the household activity. Their working conditions and living environment are hazardous to their health.

For studying the socio-economic development of minorities, it is essential to understand the social, economic, educational, health and living conditions of the target population and identify various problems that the community has been facing. A number of programmes initiated for socio-economic development of the poor, e.g., the Integrated Rural Development Programme (IRDP), Drought Prone Area Programme (DPAP) and the Jawahar Rozgar Yojana (JRY) have been in operation in the state for quite some time. The Training of Rural Youth for Self-Employment Programme (TRYSEM) provides productive self-employment opportunities to unemployed rural youth. A number of corporations, projects and training centres has been in operation for helping the artisans and skilled workers by arranging their training, supplying them raw materials and marketing their products. Minorities Finance and Development Corporation also provides financial assistance to the youth of the minority community for self-employment and some technical training for expanding job opportunities for them. It is, however, to be noted that the existence of such welfare programmes is not enough. More important is the strategy that is adopted for covering the various segments of the population. The problem of lack of enthusiasm among the minorities in participation in these programmes may be either because they are not completely relevant for them or the strategy adopted for implementing them is such that enough effort is not made to involve every segment of the target population.

It has generally been observed that the benefits of the various development programmes have been derived more by those among the poor who already had some asset base either in terms of land or small business or skills to produce easily marketable items. Those having no such endowments have not been covered and thus their skills are not effectively utilized under assistance provided under various programmes. The minority population in the state of Uttar Pradesh is observed to have somewhat different pattern in this regard from the general population. The landless and unskilled constitute a smaller proportion, while the skilled (artisans) and those engaged in household business would form a larger proportion among them than in the general population. Those engaged in the traditional occupations with the help of some asset and skill endowment constitute a sizeable population among them. As such, it is expected that the major programmes which have a bias in favour of such groups should have benefitted the minorities to a larger extent than the general population. It is, therefore, worth examining the status of minorities - the level of their participation and the benefits they have derived from these programmes.

For the speedy development of the minority population and the strategy required to be adopted for improving their conditions, we propose to study the working and the impact of various existing programmes and measures. Besides identifying the areas which need modifications in the existing programmes, we also propose to identify the areas which need new programmes. The frame of our study provides for approaching the problem from the 'population end' rather than from the 'programme end'.

All the programmes, therefore, which have been in operation from time to time, will get covered in the actual study.

As for educational conditions of minorities, a number of studies indicate that education has not received priority in most of their households. They are not only behind other communities in enrolment in schools but their proportion among dropouts is also higher and their performance in examinations is poorer. The proportion of minority students in technical and higher education is very low.

It is widely believed that due to poor economic and living conditions, use of non-potable water, illiteracy and unhygienic and insanitary surroundings, a large proportion of the minority suffers from poor health conditions. There is also lack of concern for the consequences of such conditions especially with regard to their impact on maternal and child health. Consequently, mortality rates among infants and toddlers are significantly higher. Generally, the health conditions of minority are poor as various types of ailments are common. A significant proportion of them suffers from various ailments particularly, tuberculosis, eye ailments and other types of diseases.

For maintaining social harmony and health, it is essential that the people in general and youth in particular have some sort of organization for conducting cultural activities and other programmes. Such activities may be useful, as they will prevent them from undesirable activities during their free time. Further, through such activities the people may be communicated about a number of opportunities, facilities and programmes that are available for their upliftment.

Programmes for youth particularly those for the under-employed and the unemployed which can engage them for improving their skills can help them in developing their employment opportunities are important view point of their economic conditions. The youth power can also be channelised for accelerating a number of welfare schemes for which they can be used as participants and promoters, such as, Total Literacy Campaign, Immunization Campaign, etc. They can also be enrolled as volunteers by the organizations such as the Nehru Yuva Kendras. Thus, they can be utilized through a number of programmes and activities of the government and the NGOs.

It is obvious that socio-economic conditions of minority community are pitiable and thus there is an urgent need to adopt appropriate measures for their socio-economic development. The present study is a modest attempt towards this direction with following specific objectives:

Objectives of the Study

1. To empirically examine the level of education, enrolment, non-enrolment and dropout among minority students;
2. To understand the employment structure and poverty profile of minorities;
3. To study the general characteristics of housing, health conditions, medical facilities and sanitation available to minority communities;
4. To study the extent to which various developmental programmes and schemes, have benefited the minorities engaged in various economic activities;
5. To identify factors inhibiting the growth of entrepreneurship among minorities;
6. To study the role of the Minorities Finance and Development Corporation for improving the economic conditions of minorities;
7. To find out the availability and the standard of the coaching for minority youths for competitive examinations;

8. To identify the activities in which the youth students, unemployed and the under-employed may be engaged during their free time and the use of common community assets by minorities;
9. To find out the extent to which benefits from training may reach to minority communities in their specific areas; and
10. To provide certain specific policy recommendations relevant for socio-economic development for minorities on the basis of general findings of the study.

Rampur District: Origin and Background

Present study relates to Rampur district. Historically, the origin of Rampur district goes back to 1774. It was named after headquarter town of Rampur, which was identified as a seat of Rohilla power. This was considered to be earlier period when the Treaty of Laldhang was concluded between the Nawab Wazir of Awadh and the Rohillog in 1774. Traditionally, the site of the town was a group of four villages, which was known as Rampur. Present Rampur town is said to have been founded by Faizullah Khan in 1775. Faizullah Khan first called it Faizabad. Thereafter, it was changed to Mustafabad urf Rampur. Presently, Rampur is found in the old records of the district. On December 1, 1942, the Rampur district was created from the erstwhile Rampur state.[1]

The district Rampur is placed at the central part of the northern half of Rohilkhand division. It lies between Lat. 28°25' N and 29°10' N and between Long. 78°51' E to 79°28' E. The extreme length of the Rampur is about 81 kms. from North to South, while 49 kms. from East to West.[2] The district is almost heart shaped, which is bounded by Nainital district in the North, Badaun on the South, Bareilly on the East and Moradabad on the West. The district is spread over the area of 2367 sq. kms. and is smallest district in terms of covered area in the state of Uttar Pradesh.

Rampur district consists of 5 Tehsils, i.e. (1) Swar, (2) Bilaspur, (3) Shahbad, (4) Milak and (5) Rampur Sadar. In 1993-94, there were 75 Nyaya Panchayats and 742 Gram Sabhas. The Rampur district consists of 5 municipalities, i.e. (1) Tanda, (2) Bilaspur, (3) Swar, (4) Milak and (5) Rampur. It has 6 development blocks, i.e. (1) Swar, (2) Bilaspur, (3) Saidnagar, (4) Chamaraua, (5) Shahbad and (6) Milak. According to 1991 Census, the district consists of 1153 total villages, of which inhabitated villages are 1098. The total population of the district according to 1991 census was to 15.02 lakhs, of which, 73.86 per cent were rural and 26.14 per cent were urban. Across different religions, 47.90 per cent of population were Hindu, 47.95 per cent Muslim, 0.48 per cent Christian, 3.57 per cent Sikhs and 0.10 per cent were others. In the district, in 1981, 54.50 per cent of population were males, while to 45.50 per cent females. Within the rural area, 55 per cent of population were males and to 45 per cent females. In the urban area, 53.11 per cent of population were males, while to 46.89 per cent females.[3]

In 1991, of the total population of the district, 25.40 per cent were literates, while to 74.60 per cent illiterates. Within the literates, 33.80 per cent were males, while to 15.3 per cent females. In 1993-94, the number of junior basic schools per one lakh population was 52.7; senior basic schools to 8.7; higher secondary schools to 2.8; and Degree College to 0.9. Also, in 1993-94, there was one branch of commercial bank, out of 17,858 of population. Out of one lakh of population in the district, there were equal number of allopathic hospitals and primary health centres (4). The size of household in 1991 was worked out to be 6.49 in the district, being to 6.48 in rural and to 6.74 in urban areas. The district is agriculturally rich. In 1991, of the total main workers, 57.10 per cent were cultivators,

15.50 per cent wage earners, while to 6.10 per cent were employed in trade and commerce, 7.50 per cent in non-household industry and to 1.70 per cent in household industry. Workers employed in construction come to 1.20 per cent, in transport and communication to 2.70 per cent and those in other economic activities to 7.70 per cent. In 1988-89, the district had 118 registered factories, of which 70 were at functioning condition. The average daily employees were found to be 10,262 in the district.[4]

The different occupations were carried out by different castes. Goldsmithy was carried out by Sonars, tailoring by Darjis, scavengers by Bhanjis, trading by Vaishyas, shoe making by Mochis and sweet making by Halwais. Other castes which adopted traditional occupations were Julaha who were engaged in weaving; Barhais in carpentry; Gadariyas as shepherds; and Kachhis as market gardners. Many others who also pursued occupations were hawkers, pedlars, bidi makers, knife makers, rickshaw drivers, animal drawn vehicle drivers, carpet makers, furnishers, photographers, astrologers, basket weavers, etc.[5]

Methodology and Data Base

The present study is based on the information collected from secondary and primary sources. We, however, understand that adequate secondary data pertaining to different aspects on the conditions of minorities may not be available at the district level. Thus, for the status study we propose to collect information from the primary sources. The objective behind the collection of the data from the primary sources is the virtual non-existence of information from the secondary sources. The survey of the sample population is mainly to identify the various factors/reasons for economic backwardness of the minorities in different walkS of life.

In order to understand the problems of minorities, such as, educational backwardness, economic backwardness, poor health conditions, dismal living conditions, etc. 500 minority households from the Rampur district have been selected. This is done because data on minorities at block or at village level has not been found available from the secondary sources. It would not only reveal the actual socio-economic conditions of minorities, but also would provide a strong support in the absence of data from the secondary sources.

1. Method Used for Selecting the Minority Households

A multi-stage sampling procedure has been followed for selecting the minority households. As per census 1991, there were 52 per cent of minority population in the district, of which 47.95 per cent were Muslims, 3.57 per cent Sikhs and to 0.48 per cent the Christian population. It is given in Table I.1.

TABLE I.1

Religion-wise Distribution of Minority Population to Total District Population: Rampur, 1991

Religion	*Percentage to total district population*
Muslim	47.95
Sikh	3.57
Christian	0.48
Total	52.00

Source: Census of India, 1991.

Among the total minority population, 92.20 per cent were Muslims, 6.90 per cent Sikhs and to 0.90 per cent were the Christians as given in Table I.2. Owing to non-availability of information on households from different groups of minorities, this was considered as the appropriate base for distributing the 500 households among different minority groups. At the first stage of sampling, of the 500 households proposed to be selected, 92.20 per cent or 460 households were selected from Muslims, 6.90 per cent or 35 households from Sikhs and to 0.90 per cent or 5 households from Christian community in the district. It is given below in Table I.3.

TABLE I.2

Religion-wise Distribution of Minority Population to Total Minority Population: Rampur, 1991

Religion	*Percentage to total minority population*
Muslim	92.20
Sikh	6.90
Christian	0.90
Total	100.00

Source: Census of India, 1991.

TABLE I.3

Selection of Minorities in Rampur District : 1991

Minority	*Percentage to total minority population*	*Households selected for survey (No.)*
Muslim	92.2	460
Sikh	6.90	35
Christian	0.90	5
Total	100.00	500

Source: Census of India, 1991.

Selected households from different minority groups were further bifurcated into rural and urban areas. This was done in proportion to population in different minority groups available at the district level. At the second stage, as shown in Table I.4, of 460 Muslim households proposed for the study, 62.72 per cent or 290 Muslim households were selected from rural, while to 37.28 per cent or 170 from the urban areas. A similar method has also been adopted for selecting the Sikhs and Christian households. Of the 35 Sikh households to be surveyed, 91.47 per cent or 32 Sikh's households were selected from rural, while to 8.53 per cent or 3 households from the urban areas. Similarly, of the 5 Christian households to be surveyed, 87.19 per cent or 4 were chosen from rural, while to 12.81 per cent or 1 household from the urban areas in the district (Table I.4). Thus, of the 500 minority households, 326 have been drawn from the rural and to 174 from the urban areas from the Rampur district.

TABLE I.4

Distribution of Minority Population into Rural and Urban Areas: Rampur, 1991

Items	*Rural*	*Urban*	*Total*
Percentage of Muslim to total Muslim population in Rampur	62.72	37.28	100.00
Muslim households selected for survey (No.)	290.00	170.00	460.00
Per cent of Sikh population to total Sikh population in Rampur	91.47	8.53	100.00
Sikh households selected for survey (No.)	32.00	3.00	35.00
Percentage of Christian population to total Christian population in Rampur	87.19	12.81	100.00
Christian households selected for survey (No.)	4.00	1.00	5.00
Total households from minorities selected for survey (No.)	326.00	174.00	500.00

Source: Census of India, 1991.

Subsequently, 322 minority households from rural areas were broken down into blocks and villages. This is partly based on the relative significance of Muslim and Sikh households across the 2 blocks and 10 villages as partly revealed by the Department of Minority Welfare and partly by the secondary sources of information. The sample of 4 Christian households has, however, not been included in the total sample of households (326) to be selected from rural areas spread over into 10 villages and to 2 blocks of Rampur district. These 4 Christian households have been separately surveyed randomly from another selected village of (Swar and Bilaspur blocks) of the Rampur district.

Thus, the sample of households drawn from Muslim and Sikh households from rural areas was restricted to 322 and not to 326. Hence, sample of households from Muslims and Sikhs as portrayed in table I.5 are 322 from rural areas of Rampur district.

Based on above procedure, two blocks i.e., Bilaspur and Swar and from each block 5 villages were selected for drawing the sample of minority households from rural areas. At the third stage, a sample of Muslim and Sikh households has been drawn from rural areas of Swar and Bilaspur blocks. The distribution of Muslim and Sikh households into two blocks is based on the existing Muslim and Sikh households in 5 villages in each block. Based on this procedure, out of 1169, 196 Muslim households from Swar and out of 562, 94 Muslim households from Bilaspur block have been selected.

TABLE I.5

Selection of Households from Minorities from the Blocks in Rampur District

Block	*Muslim households*		*Sample households*	*Sikh households*		*Sample households*
	Number	*Percentage*	*Number*	*Number*	*Percentage*	*Number*
Swar*	1169	67.53	196	23	24.73	8
Bilaspur*	562	32.47	94	70	75.27	24
Total	1731	100.00	290	93	100.00	32

Note: Sample of 4 Christian households has not been included as these have been chosen from non-selected village in Bilaspur block of Rampur district.

* Based on the information for 5 villages and do not represent the total information of selected blocks of Swar and Bilaspur.

Source: Records supplied by Election Office, District Rampur, 1996.

Similarly, of the 23 Sikh's households, 8 households from Swar and out of 70, 24 households from Bilaspur have been selected for in-depth investigation. It is recorded in Table I.5. From these two blocks, 5 villages from each block have been selected. Selected villages are: (1) Narpat Nagar, (2) Raipur, (3) Mundwa Hasanpur, (4) Meerapur Meerganj and (5) Milak Dundi from Swar, while (1) Ahro, (2) Godhi, (3) Dhavani Hasanur, (4) Tal Mahavar, and (5) Kuiya from Bilaspur block have been selected (Tables I.6 and I.7).

Electoral record available from Election Office has been used as a basis for identifying the Muslim and Sikh households in the selected villages. As per electoral record, 439 Muslims in Narpat Nagar, 330 in Raipur, 165 in Mundwa Hasanpur, 145 in Mirapur Meerganj and 90 Muslim households in Milak Dundi existed in Swar block. In all, 1169 Muslim households existed in 5 selected villages of Swar block. Similarly, there were 23 Sikh households, of which, 8 were in Mirapur Meerganj; 6 in Raipur; 5 in Narpat Nagar; and 4 in Mundwa Hasanpur in Swar block. However, there were no Sikh's households in Milak Dundi in this block (Table I.6).

TABLE I.6

Selection of Minority Households from Villages from Swar Block in Rampur District

Villages	*Muslim households*		*Muslim households selected*	*Sikh households*		*Sikh households selected*
	Number	*Percentage*	*Number*	*Number*	*Percentage*	*Number*
Narpat Nagar	439	37.56	74	5	21.74	2
Raipur	330	28.23	55	6	26.09	2
Mandwa Hasanpur	165	14.11	28	4	17.39	1
Meerapur Meerganj	145	12.40	24	8	34.78	3
Milak Dundi	90	7.70	15	--	--	--
Total	1169	100.00	196	23	100.00	8

Source: Based on the records supplied by the Election Office, Rampur, 1996.

A similar information has also been collected from electoral records of 5 selected villages in Bilaspur block. In this block, there were 562 Muslim households, of which, 170 were in Ahro, 147 in Godhi, 113 in Dhavani Hasanpur, 74 in Tal Mahavar and 58 in Kuiya (Table I.7).

TABLE I.7

Selection of Minority Households from Villages from Bilaspur Block in Rampur District

Villages	*Muslim households*		*Muslim households selected*	*Sikh households*		*Sikh households selected*
	Number	*Percentage*	*Number*	*Number*	*Percentage*	*Number*
Ahro	170	30.24	28	--	--	--
Godhi	147	26.16	25	16	22.86	5
Dhawani Hasanpur	113	20.11	19	--	--	--
Tal Mahavar	74	13.17	12	32	45.71	11
Kuiya	58	13.17	10	22	31.43	8
Total	562	100.00	94	70	100.00	24

Source: Based on the records supplied by Election Office, Rampur, 1996.

Sample was further broken down into Muslim and Sikh households at the village level. Giving Weightage to the number households, at the fourth stage of sampling, 74 Muslim households, out of 439 and 2 Sikh households, out of 5 from Narpat Nagar; 55 Muslim households, out of 330; and to 2 Sikh households, out of 6, from Raipur; 28 Muslim households, out of 165 and 1 Sikh household, out of 4 from Mundwa Hasanpur; 24 Muslim households, out of 145 and 3 Sikh households, out of 8 from Meerapur Meerganj; and 15 Muslim households, out of 90 from Milak Dundi were selected from the Swar block. In Milak Dundi, however, the Sikh households were found non-existent (Table I.6).

Similarly from 5 villages of Bilaspur block, a sample

of Muslim and Sikh households was drawn. For instance, 28 Muslim households, out of 170 from Ahro; 25 Muslim households, out of 147 and 5 Sikh's households, out of 16 from Godhi; 19 Muslim households, out of 113 from Dhavani Hasanpur; 12 Muslim households, out of 74 and 11 Sikh's households, out of 32 from Tal Mahavar; and to 10 Muslim households, out of 58 and 8 Sikh's households, out of 22 from Kuiya village were selected (Table I.7). Finally, at the fifth stage of sampling, households so chosen has been selected from each village by using the random sampling method. This has been done in a manner that Muslim and Sikh's households from different economic activities are not disturbed.

TABLE I.8

Selection of Muslim Households from Cities in Rampur District

City	*Percentage of Muslim households engaged in main economic activities*	*Muslim households selected (Number)*
Rampur	75.86	132
Swar	24.14	42
Total	100.00	174

Source: Based on the opinion expressed by the staff members of District Minority Welfare Office, Rampur, 1997 and B.D.O. and residents of Swar Block, 1997.

As for the selection of urban households from minorities, we approached the Department of Minority Welfare, where we came to know that Rampur and the Swar were the two most important cities in Rampur district. Based on the importance of Muslim households employed in different economic activities as reported by the Department of Minority Welfare, Collectorate, Rampur and Swar have been selected for drawing the sample of Muslim households. We are told that 75.86 per cent of Muslim households were engaged in various economic activities in Rampur, while

25 per cent in Swar, if these two cities are considered together. Based on this, at the first stage, we decided to select, of the 174 Muslim households, 75.86 per cent of Muslim households or 132 households from Rampur City and to 24.14 per cent or 42 Muslim households from Swar city. Thus, 132 Muslim households from Rampur city and to 42 Muslim households from Swar city were selected. It has been described in Table I.8.

It was thought that it would be more appropriate if selected urban Muslim households were drawn from different economic activities. This was done on the basis of relative importance of Muslim households employed in various economic activities in Rampur district. In case of Swar, we relied on the similar information provided by the Block Development Officer, Swar. The information provided by B.D.O. Swar was further verified from the few experts, residing in the Swar city since 15 years. Selection of Muslim households from these two cities across various economic activities are presented in Tables I.9 and I.10.

TABLE I.9

Selection of Muslim Households from Major Economic Activities in Rampur City: 1997

Activity	*Muslim households selected*	
	Per cent	*Number*
1. Manufacturing and trading of food products	**5.00**	**6**
1.1 Biscuit making and selling	5.00	6
2. Manufacturing and trading of leather and leather goods	**3.00**	**4**
3. Manufacturing and selling of furniture	**2.00**	**3**
4. Manufacturing and trading of engineering goods	**17.00**	**22**
4.1 Manufacturing and selling of garden tools	5.00	6
4.2 Manufacturing and selling of knife and cutlery products	7.00	9

4.3 Selling of electronic products and parts	3.00	4
4.4 Selling of electrical products and parts	2.00	3
5. Manufacturing and trading of paper products	**5.00**	**6**
5.1 Making and selling of kites	5.00	6
6. Manufacturing and trading of textile products	**37.00**	**47**
6.1 Selling of readymade garments	5.00	6
6.2 Making and selling of caps	5.00	6
6.3 Stitching work and embroidery work on readymade garments and zari work	27.00	35
7. Self employed services	**15.00**	**19**
7.1 PCO	3.00	4
7.2 Self-employed in transport services	7.00	9
7.3 Self-employed in repairing work	5.00	6
8. Others not specified	**16.00**	**21**
8.1 Making and selling of bidies	9.00	12
8.2 Trading	5.00	6
8.3 Manufacturing and selling of glass and brass products	2.00	3
Total (1, 2, 3, 4, 5, 6, 7 & 8)	**100.00**	**128**

Note: It may be mentioned that 3 Sikhs and 1 Christian households have not been selected from major economic activities in Rampur city as shown in the above table. These have, however, been selected randomly from other economic activities from Rampur city.

It is interesting to note that a majority of Muslim households in Rampur city is found engaged in manufacturing and trading of textiles (37 per cent) followed by engineering goods (17 per cent), others (16 per cent) and bidi making (9%).

Thus, based on the importance of different economic activities, 128 Muslim households have been selected from different economic activities from Rampur city. In Swar city, bidi making and selling of bidi activity has employed 52 per cent of Muslim households, while self-employed services to 26 per cent of Muslim households. Thus, at the second stage, selection of Muslim households from Rampur and Swar is done by using random sampling procedure, and due attention is paid to select the Muslim households from different geographical regions and economic activities.

TABLE I.10

Selection of Muslim Households from Major Economic Activities in Swar City: 1997

Activity	*Muslim households selected*	
	Per cent	*Number*
1. Manufacturing and trading of wood products	**5.00**	**2**
2. Manufacturing and trading of engineering goods	**7.00**	**3**
2.1 Manufacturing and selling of agricultural tools	3.00	1
2.2 Selling of electronic products and parts	2.00	1
2.3 Selling of electrical products and parts	2.00	1
3. Manufacturing and selling of textile products	**10.00**	**4**
3.1 Stitching and embroidery work on readymade garments	10.00	4
4. Self-employed services	**26.00**	**11**
4.1 Self-employed in tailoring	7.00	3
4.2 Self-employed in transport services	2.00	1
4.3 Self-employed in repairing work	10.00	4
4.4 Hair cutting and cloth washing	7.00	3
5. Others not specified	**52.00**	**22**
5.1 Making and selling of bidies	15.00	6
5.2 Trading not specified elsewhere	37.00	16
Total (1, 2, 3, 4 & 5)	**100.00**	**42**

Source: Based on the opinion expressed by the Block Development Officer and Experts residing in Swar city of the Rampur district, 1997.

For the purpose of study one set of structured questionnaire was prepared for minority respondents, incorporating various relevant questions on socio-economic conditions of minorities spread over in selected villages and blocks of Rampur district. The structured questionnaire schedule was administered by the efficient and trained research personnel on the heads of selected families of minorities. The actual field work was started in May 1997, which was completed in August 1997. Selection of the blocks, villages, urban localities and the sample was done prior to actual field work. The information of the present study relates to 1996-97.

Plan of the Study

Following this introductory Chapter I, Chapter II aims at discussing the social conditions of minorities. Chapter III discusses the economic aspects of minorities. Chapter IV has been devoted to discuss the housing and health conditions. It discusses the general conditions of housing, health, medical facilities and sanitation available to minority community and their requirements. Chapter V explores benefits of new economic activities in terms of employment, earnings and marketing. Besides, it also discusses as to how the fruits of rural development programmes are shared by the minority households. Also, it identifies the various activities in which youth students, unemployed and the under-employed are likely to be engaged during their free time. Chapter VI finally provides certain specific policy recommendations for the development of minorities based on the general findings of the study.

REFERENCES

1. *Gazetteer of India,* Government of Uttar Pradesh, Department of District Gazetteer, U.P., 1974.
2. *Ibid.*
3. Department of Economics and Statistics, State Planning Institute, U.P., *Statistical Bulletin,* District Rampur, 1994.
4. Department of Economics and Statistics, State Planning Institute, U.P., *Statistical Bulletin,* District Rampur, 1994.
5. *Gazetteer of India,* Government of Uttar Pradesh, Department of District Gazetteer, U.P., 1974.

2

Social Characteristics of Minorities

Introduction

Present chapter examines the various social characteristics of minorities in Rampur district. In particular, an attempt is made to examine empirically: (i) religion-wise and caste-wise distribution of minority households, (ii) marital status, (iii) educational background and (iv) enrolment, drop-out and non-enrolment of minorities. The examination on these aspects has been considered important because these will likely to provide the basic guidelines for the socio-cconomic development of minorities.

Distribution of Minorities by Castes

1. Rural Areas

Table II.1 classifies minority households by castes. In Bilaspur block, there are 30 minority respondents in Godhi, of which 10 (or 33.33 per cent) are from general, while 20 (or 66.67 per cent) belong to backward caste. In Ahro village, there are 28 minority households of which 17 (or 60.71 per cent) belong to general, while to 11 (or 39.29 per cent) to backward caste. In Tal Mahavar, there are 23 minority households, of which 21 (or 91.30 per cent) belong to backward, while to 2 (or 8.70 per cent) to backward caste category. In Kuiya, there are 18 minority households, of which 11 (or 61.11 per cent) are from general, while 7 (or 38.89 per cent) from backward caste community. In the Dhavani Hasanpur, there are19 minority respondents, of

TABLE II.1

Distribution of Minority Households in Rural and Urban Areas by Castes: Rampur, 1997

Block / Village	*Caste-wise distribution of minority households*		
	General	*Backward*	*All*
	Rural		
A. Bilaspur			
Ahro	17(60.71)	11(39.29)	28(100.00)
Dhavani Hasanpur	16(84.21)	3(15.79)	19(100.00)
Godhi	10(33.33)	20(66.67)	30(100.00)
Kuiya	11(61.11)	7(38.89)	18(100.00)
Tal Mahavar	21(91.30)	2(8.70)	23(100.00)
Isa Nagar	4(100.0)	--	4(100.00)
Sub-Total (A)	**79(64.75)**	**43(35.25)**	**122(100.00)**
B. Swar			
Mandawa Hasanpur	29(100.0)	--	29(100.00)
Raipur	47(82.46)	10(17.54)	57(100.00)
Mirapur Meerganj	27(100.0)	--	27(100.00)
Milak Dundi	8(53.33)	7(46.67)	15(100.00)
Narpat Nagar	67(88.16)	9(11.84)	76(100.00)
Sub-Total (B)	**178(87.25)**	**26(12.75)**	**204(100.00)**
Rural (A+B)	**257(78.83)**	**69(21.17)**	**326(100.00)**
	Urban Cities		
(C) Rampur	93(70.45)	39(29.55)	132(100.00)
(D) Swar	17(40.48)	25(59.52)	42(100.00)
Sub-Total (C+D)	**110(63.22)**	**64(36.78)**	**174(100.00)**
Grand Total (Rural+Urban)	**367(73.40)**	**133(26.60)**	**500(100.00)**

Note: Figures within denote per cent to row total.

Source: Based on the data collected from the field.

which 16 (or 84.21 per cent) are from general, while rest 3 (or 15.79 per cent) from the backward caste. In Isa Nagar village, there are 4 minority households and all of them belong to general caste category. In 6 villages of Bilaspur block, there exist 122 minority households, of which 79 (or 64.75 per cent) belong to general caste, while to 43 (or 35.25 per cent) to backward caste category.

Swar block consists of 5 villages, i.e., Narpat Nagar, Raipur, Mandawa Hasanpur, Mirapur Meerganj and Milak Dundi. In Narpat Nagar, there are 76 respondents from minority community, of which 67 (or 88.16 per cent) are from general, while to 9 (or 11.84 per cent) from the backward caste. In Raipur, there are 57 minority households, of which 47 (or 82.46 per cent) are from general, while to 10 (or 17.54 per cent) are from the backward caste. In Mandwa Hasanpur, there exists 29 minority households and all of them belong to general caste category. In Mirapur Meerganj, there are 27 minority households and all of them belong to general caste category. In Milak Dundi, there are 15 households, of which 8 (or 53.33 per cent) belong to general, while to 7 (or 46.67 per cent) to backward caste category.

In all 5 villages of Swar block, there are 204 minority households, of which, 178 (or 87.25 per cent) belong to general caste, while 26 (or 12.75 per cent) to backward caste category. In all 11 villages of Bilaspur and Swar blocks, there exits 326 minority households, of which 257 (or 78.83 per cent) belong to general, while to 69 (or 21.17 per cent) to backward caste category. Thus, general caste is found more significant as compared to backward caste in rural areas.

2. Urban Areas

We may now discuss the caste-wise distribution of minority households in cities of Rampur and Swar in Rampur district. There are 132 minority households in Rampur city, of which, 93 (or 70.45 per cent) are from general, while to 39 (or 29.55 per cent) are from the backward caste. In Swar, there are 42 minority households, of which, 25 (or 59.52 per cent) belong to backward, while 17 (or 40.48 per cent) to general caste category.

In Rampur and Swar cities together, there are 174 minority households, of which 110 (or 63.22 per cent) are from general, while to 64 (or 36.78 per cent) from the backward caste category. In rural and urban total, out of 500, minority households 367 (or 73.40 per cent) are from the general, while 133 (or 26.60 per cent) from the backward caste category. Thus, general caste has been found more significant as compared to backward caste in the Rampur district (Table II.1).

Minority Population By Age

1. Rural Areas

Table II.2 classifies minority population by different age groups, such as, less than 15 years, 15 to 24 years, 25 to 39 years, 40 to 59 years and to more than 60 years in Bilaspur and Swar blocks spread over across 11 villages. In Godhi, 46.02 per cent of minority population are found to less than 15 years of age, while that in Kuiya to 41.51 per cent. The corresponding minority household members in reference age group are found to be 33.49 per cent in Ahro; 30.47 per cent in Dhavani Hasanpur; 25.64 per cent in Talmahavar and to 11.76 per cent in Isa Nagar. Similarly, minority population within the age group of 15 to 24 years are found to be 35.15 per cent in Dhavani Hasanpur; 30.13 per cent in Tal Mahavar; 29.41 per cent in Isa Nagar; 25.84 per cent in Ahro; 22.64 per cent in Kuiya; and to 19.03 per cent in Godhi. Minority population within the age group of 25 years to 39 years are found to be 38.24 per cent in Isanagar, 24.21 per cent in Godhi; 19.14 per cent in Ahro; 18.87 per cent in Kuiya; 17.95 per cent in Tal Mahavar; and to 10.94 per cent in Dhavani Hasanpur. Minority population within age group of 40 years to 59 years are found highest in Tal Mahavar (19.23 per cent), while lowest in Godhi (9.73 per cent). Similarly, minority population within the age group of 60 years and above are found to be highest in Tal Mahavar (7.05 per cent), while lowest in Kuiya (1.89 per cent).

In all six villages of Bilaspur block, a relatively younger persons belonging under the age of 15 years are found more significant, which have accounted for over 35 per cent of the minority population. The proportion of minority population falling beyond age group of <15 years is found less significant in Bilaspur block. Thus, this block is dominated significantly by the youngsters.

In Swar block, the minority population within the age group of < 15 years, has been found to be 50 per cent in Mirapur Meerganj; 45.30 per cent in Narpat Nagar; 44.62 per cent in Raipur; 41.76 per cent in Milak Dundi; and to 37.65 per cent in Mandwa Hasanpur. Minority population falling within the age group of 60 years and above has been found to be lowest in all villages. In all 5 villages of Swar block, the population within the age group of <15 years is found to be 44.26 per cent; 15 to 24 years to 16.07 per cent; 25 to 39 years to 22.31 per cent; 40 to 59 years to 16.07 per cent and 60 and above to 1.29 per cent. However, minority population within the age group of 60 years and above is found to be of least significance. Thus, this block is also seen dominated relatively more by the youngsters.

In two blocks (Bilaspur and Swar) spread over in 11 villages, 40.20 per cent of minority population are found below the age group of 15 years; 20.43 per cent between 15 to 24 years; 20.84 per cent between 25 to 39 years; 15.71 per cent between 40 to 59 years; and to 2.82 per cent in the age group of 60 years and above. Thus, in rural areas, relatively young persons are found relatively more significant than the others (Table II.2).

TABLE II.2

Distribution of Minority Population by Different Age Groups in Rural and Urban Areas: Rampur, 1997

Block / Village / Cities	*Age group*					
	<15 years (No.)	*15-24 years (No.)*	*25-39 years (No.)*	*40-59 years (No.)*	*60 years & Above (No.)*	*Total minority population (No.)*
			Rural			
A. Bilaspur						
Ahro	70(33.49)	54(25.84)	40(19.14)	35(16.75)	10(4.78)	209(100.00)
Dhavani Hasanpur	39(30.47)	45(35.15)	14(10.94)	23(17.97)	7(5.47)	128(100.00)
Godhi	104(46.02)	43(19.03)	48(21.24)	22(9.73)	9(3.98)	226(100.00)
Kuiya	44(41.51)	24(22.64)	20(13.87)	16(15.09)	2(1.89)	106(100.00)
Tal Mahavar	40(25.64)	47(30.13)	28(17.95)	30(19.23)	11(7.05)	156(100.00)
Isa Nagar	4(11.76)	10(29.41)	13(38.24)	5(14.71)	2(5.88)	34(100.00)
Sub-Total (A)	**301(35.04)**	**223(25.96)**	**163(13.98)**	**131(15.25)**	**41(4.77)**	**859(100.00)**
B. Swar						
Mandawa Hasanpur	64(37.65)	21(12.35)	36(21.18)	38(22.35)	11(6.47)	170(100.00)
Raipur	141(44.62)	72(22.79)	49(15.51)	53(16.77)	1(0.31)	316(100.00)
Mirapur Meerganj	75(50.00)	23(15.33)	33(22.00)	19(12.67)	- -	150(100.00)
Milak Dundi	38(41.76)	20(21.98)	15(16.48)	17(18.68)	1(1.10)	91(100.00)

Age group *Block / Village / Cities*	*<15 years (No.)*	*15-24 years (No.)*	*25-39 years (No.)*	*40-59 years (No.)*	*60 years & Above (No.)*	*Total minority population (No.)*
Narpat Nagar	164(45.30)	39(10.77)	110(30.39)	48(13.26)	1(0.28)	362(100.00)
Sub-Total (B)	**482(44.26)**	**175(16.07)**	**243(22.31)**	**175(16.07)**	**14(1.29)**	**1089(100.00)**
Rural (A+B)	**783(40.20)**	**398(20.43)**	**406(20.84)**	**306(15.71)**	**55(2.82)**	**1948(100.00)**
			Urrban Cities			
(C) Rampur	265(31.74)*	218(26.11)*	179(21.43)*	148(17.73)*	25(2.99)*	835(100.00)
(D) Swar	85(42.29)	21(10.45)	61(30.35)	32(15.92)	2(0.99)	201(100.00)
Sub-Total (C+D)	**350(33.78)**	**239(23.07)**	**240(23.17)**	**180(17.37)**	**27(2.61)**	**1036(100.00)**
Grand Total **(Rural+Urban)**	**1133(37.97)**	**637(21.34)**	**646(21.65)**	**486(16.29)**	**82(2.75)**	**2984(100.00)**

* Indicates only Christian households.

Note: Figures within parentheses denote percent to total minority population.

Source: Based on the data collected from the villages in Bilaspur and Swar blocks and from Rampur and Swar cities in Rampur District.

2. Urban Areas

We may now discuss the minority population belonging to different age-groups in urban areas. This is given in Table II.2 in Rampur and Swar cities. In Rampur, around 32 per cent of minority population are found below the age group of 15 years. At the bottom is the old persons falling in the age group of 60 years and above, which are found to be about 3 per cent in the Rampur city. In Swar, minority population to below 15 years of age are found over 42 per cent, while those of 60 years and above are about 1 per cent. In these two cities combined, a minority of population falling to less than 15 years of age has been found to be highest being to 34 per cent, while those of 60 years and above are the lowest being to 2.61 per cent. Thus, urban areas are also seen dominated by young non-adult population (Table II.2).

In rural and urban areas combined, around 38 per cent of minority population are found below the age of 15 years, while around 3 per cent are in the age group of 60 years and above (Table II.2). The empirical finding, thus, suggests that Rampur district has largely been dominated by non-adult population, being to 40.20 per cent in rural than that in urban areas of 33.78 per cent.

Marital Status of the Minority Population and the Size of Household

1. Rural Areas

Table II.3 gives the marital status of the minority population. In Bilaspur block, a majority of males is found unmarried (61.34 per cent), while in Ahro village, 48.89 per cent of females are found married. Thus, a majority of the population is found unmarried (55.50 per cent). In Dhavani Hasanpur, a majority of males is found unmarried (56.34 per cent), while females married (50.88 per cent). In this village, a majority of population is found unmarried (51.56 per cent). In Godhi, a majority of males is found

TABLE II.3

Marital Status of Family Members in Rural and Urban Areas: Rampur, 1997

Block / Village / Cities	Males					Females					Total				
	Married (No.)	Unmarried (No.)	Widdow/widower (No.)	Divorcee (No.)	Sub-Total (No.)	Married (No.)	Unmarried (No.)	Widdow/widower (No.)	Divorcee (No.)	Sub-Total (No.)	Married (No.)	Unmarried (No.)	Widdow/widower (No.)	Divorcee (No.)	Sub-Total (No.)
Rural															
A. Bilaspur															
Ahro	44(36.98)	73(61.43)	1(0.84)	1(0.84)	119(100.0)	44(48.89)	43(47.78)	3(3.83)	--	90(100.0)	88(42.11)	116(55.50)	4(1.91)	1(0.48)	209(100.0)
Dhavani Hasanpur	29(40.85)	40(56.34)	2(2.81)	--	71(100.0)	29(50.88)	26(45.61)	2(3.51)	--	57(100.0)	58(45.31)	66(51.56)	4(3.13)	--	128(100.0)
Godhi	49(36.84)	83(62.41)	1(0.75)	--	133(100.0)	49(52.69)	42(45.16)	2(2.15)	--	93(100.0)	98(43.36)	125(55.31)	3(1.33)	--	226(100.0)
Kuiya	20(35.71)	33(58.93)	3(5.36)	--	56(100.0)	20(40.00)	29(58.00)	1(2.00)	--	50(100.0)	40(37.74)	62(58.49)	4(3.77)	--	106(100.0)
Tal Mahavar	36(40.91)	52(59.09)	--	--	88(100.0)	37(54.41)	27(39.71)	4(5.88)	--	68(100.0)	73(46.79)	79(50.64)	4(2.57)	--	156(100.0)
Isa Nagar	8(42.11)	11(57.89)	--	--	19(100.0)	8(53.33)	7(46.67)	--	--	15(100.0)	16(47.06)	18(52.94)	--	--	34(100.0)
Sub-Total (A)	186(38.27)	292(60.08)	7(1.44)	1(0.21)	486(100.0)	187(50.13)	174(46.65)	12(3.22)	--	373(100.0)	373(43.42)	466(54.25)	19(2.21)	1(0.12)	859(100.0)
B. Swar															
Mandawa Hasanpur	45(48.39)	47(50.54)	1(1.07)	--	93(100.0)	45(58.44)	32(41.56)	--	--	77(100.0)	90(52.94)	79(46.47)	1(0.59)	--	170(100.0)
Raipur	59(32.96)	120(67.04)	--	--	179(100.0)	59(43.07)	78(56.93)	--	--	137(100.0)	118(37.34)	198(62.66)	--	--	316(100.0)
Mirapur Meerganj	29(33.72)	57(66.28)	--	--	86(100.0)	29(45.31)	35(54.69)	--	--	64(100.0)	58(38.67)	92(61.33)	--	--	150(100.0)
Milak Dundi	15(31.25)	32(66.67)	1(2.08)	--	48(100.0)	15(34.88)	22(51.16)	6(13.96)	--	43(100.0)	30(32.97)	54(59.34)	7(7.69)	--	91(100.0)
Narpat Nagar	79(40.51)	115(58.98)	1(0.51)	--	195(100.0)	79(47.31)	80(47.90)	8(4.79)	--	167(100.0)	158(43.65)	195(53.87)	9(2.48)	--	362(100.0)
Sub-Total (B)	227(37.77)	371(61.73)	3(0.50)	--	601(100.0)	227(46.52)	247(50.61)	14(2.87)	--	488(100.0)	454(41.69)	618(56.75)	17(1.56)	--	1089(100.0)
Rural Total (A+B)	413 (38.00)	663 (60.99)	10 (0.92)	1 (0.09)	1087 (100.0)	414 (48.08)	421 (48.90)	26 (3.02)	-- --	861 (100.0)	827 (42.45)	1084 (55.64)	36 (1.85)	1 (0.05)	1948 (100.0)

Urban Cities

(C) Rampur	143(31.92)	299(66.74)	6(1.34)	- -	488(100.0)	142(36.69)	215(55.56)	30(7.75)	- -	387(100.0)	285(34.13)	514(61.56)	36(4.31)	- -	835(100.0)
(D) Swar	46(46.93)	48(48.99)	3(3.06)	1(1.02)	98(100.0)	46(44.67)	56(54.36)	1(54.36)	- -	103(100.0)	92(45.77)	104(51.74)	4(1.99)	1(0.50)	201(100.0)
Sub-Total (C+D)	189(34.62)	347(63.55)	9(1.65)	1(0.18)	546(100.0)	188(38.37)	271(55.31)	31(6.32)	- -	490(100.0)	377(36.39)	618(59.65)	40(3.86)	1(0.10)	1036(100.0)
Grand Total (Rural+Urban)	602 (36.87)	1010 (61.85)	19 (1.16)	2 (0.12)	1633 (100.0)	602 (44.56)	692 (51.22)	57 (4.22)	- - - -	1351 (100.0)	1204 (40.35)	1702 (57.04)	76 (2.55)	2 (0.06)	2984 (100.0)

* Implies only for Christian households.

Note: Figures under bracket denote per cent to sub-total of males, females and minority total.

Source: Based on the information collected from the field.

unmarried (62.41 per cent), while that of females married (52.69 per cent). It implies that a majority of minority population is unmarried (55.31 per cent). In Kuiya, a majority of males and females is found unmarried (58.93 per cent and to 58.0 per cent). In this village, a majority of minority population (58.49 per cent) is found unmarried. In Tal Mahavar, a majority of males is found unmarried (59.09 per cent), while females married (54.41 per cent). Thus, a majority of minority population (50.64 per cent) is found unmarried. In Isanagar, a majority of males (57.89 per cent) is found unmarried, while females (53.33 per cent) married. Thus, a majority of minority population (52.94 per cent) is found unmarried. In all 6 villages in Bilaspur block, it is found that a majority of males (60.08 per cent) is found unmarried, while females (50.13 per cent) married. Thus, a majority of minority population (54.25 per cent) is found unmarried.

In Swar block, the unmarried males come to 50.54 per cent in Mandwa Hasanpur; 67.04 per cent in Raipur; 66.28 per cent in Mirapur Meerganj; 66.67 per cent in Milak Dundi; and to 58.98 per cent in Narpat Nagar. In all 5 villages, 61.73 per cent of males are found unmarried. Among the females, 58.44 per cent are found married in Mandwa Hasanpur, while in remaining villages, a majority of females is found unmarried. The unmarried females come to 56.93 per cent in Raipur; 54.69 per cent in Mirapur Meerganj; 51.16 per cent in Milak Dundi; and to 47.90 per cent in Narpat Nagar. In all 5 villages in Swar block, 50.61 per cent of females are found unmarried. Thus, a majority of population in Mandwa Hasanpur is found married (52.94 per cent), while in rest of the villages, a significantly higher proportion of population is found unmarried. For instance, unmarried minority population comes to 62.66 per cent in Raipur; 61.33 per cent in Mirapur Meerganj; 59.34 per cent in Milak Dundi; and to 53.87 per cent in Narpat Nagar. In all 5 villages of Swar block, 56.75 per cent of minority population has been found unmarried. In both blocks of Bilaspur and Swar, a majority of minority population is found unmarried.

2. Urban Areas

Marital status of minority population has been recorded in Table II.3 for Rampur and Swar cities. In these two cities, a majority of males and females is found unmarried. For instance, 66.74 per cent of males in Rampur and to 48.99 per cent in Swar are found unmarried. Similarly, 55.56 per cent of females in Rampur and to 54.36 per cent in Swar city are found unmarried. Thus, in two cities 63.55 per cent of males and to 55.31 per cent of females are found unmarried.

Of the total minority population, 61.56 per cent in Rampur and to 51.74 per cent in Swar city have been found unmarried. In these two cities combined, 59.65 per cent of minority population is found unmarried (Table II.3). In rural and urban total, 61.85 per cent of males and to 51.22 per cent of females are found unmarried. In total, 57.04 per cent of minority population (male and female) are found unmarried (Table II.3). The above analysis, therefore, suggests that in selected blocks and villages of the Rampur district, unmarried minority population is relatively more significant than to those of married minority population.

3. Size of Household

3.1 Rural Areas

Table II.4 gives the number of minority families, members of families and the average size of household. In Bilaspur, the size of household comes to 8.50 in Isa Nagar, 7.53 in Godhi, 7.46 in Ahro, 6.78 in Tal Mahavar, 6.74 in Dhavani Hasanpur and in Kuiya to 5.89. In Bilaspur block, the size of household comes to 7.04. In Swar block, the size of household comes to 6.07 in Milak Dundi, 5.86 in Mandwa

Hasanpur, 5.56 in Mirapur Meerganj, 5.54 in Raipur and to 4.76 in Narpat Nagar. In Swar block, the size of household comes to 5.34 (Table II.4). Thus, in Bilaspur block, the size of household is largest in Isa Nagar, while smallest in Kuiya village. In Swar, the size of household is largest in Milak Dundi, while smallest in Narpat Nagar. Between

TABLE II.4

Household in Rural and Urban Areas: Rampur, 1997

Block / Village	*Total family (No.)*	*Total family members (No.)*	*Size of family (No.)*
		Rural	
A. Bilaspur			
Ahro	28	209	7.46
Dhavani Hasanpur	19	128	6.74
Godhi	30	226	7.53
Kuiya	18	106	5.89
Tal Mahavar	23	156	6.78
Isa Nagar	4	34	8.50
Sub-Total (A)	**122**	**859**	**7.04**
B. Swar			
Mandawa Hasanpur	29	170	5.86
Raipur	57	316	5.54
Mirapur Meerganj	27	150	5.56
Milak Dundi	15	91	6.07
Narpat Nagar	76	362	4.76
Sub-Total (B)	**.204**	**1089**	**5.34**
		Uurban	
(C) Rampur	132	835	6.33
(D) Swar	42	201	4.79
Sub-Total (Urban)	**174**	**1036**	**5.95**
Sub-Total (Rural)	**326**	**1948**	**5.98**
Grand Total	**500**	**2984**	**5.97**

Source: Based on the information collected from the field.

two blocks, the size of household is found larger in Bilaspur (7.04) than that in Swar (5.34).

3.2 Urban Areas

Table II.4 also portrays the average size of household for Rampur and Swar cities. In Rampur, the size of household comes to 6.33, while in Swar to 4.79. In Rampur and Swar cities combined, the size of household comes to 5.95. Thus, the size of household is found larger in Rampur than to that in Swar city as well as the average of urban area as a whole (Table II.4). In rural and urban total, the size of household comes to 5.97. In rural the size of household (5.98) is found larger marginally than to that in urban areas (5.95) (Table II.4).

Educational Background

1. Rural Areas

Level of literacy has been presented in Table II.5. In Bilaspur block, 22.82 per cent of minority population are found educated upto primary level; 8.50 per cent upto junior high school; 5.00 per cent upto high school; 1.75 per cent upto intermediate; 1.05 per cent upto graduation; and to 0.11 per cent upto post-graduate level. However, technical degree and diploma holders are found to be non-significant. Of the total population in Bilaspur, 60.77 per cent are found illiterates.

In Swar block, 38.84 per cent of population are found educated upto primary; 4.96 per cent upto junior high school; 2.57 per cent upto high school; 0.28 per cent upto intermediate; and to 0.09 per cent upto graduate level. Interestingly, minority population with post-graduate, technical degree and diploma are found to be non-existent. The level of illiteracy in Swar block is found to be 53.26 per cent. In both blocks of Bilaspur and Swar, 31.78 per cent of population are found educated upto primary; 6.52 per cent upto junior high school; 3.65 per cent upto high school; 0.92 per cent upto intermediate; 0.51 per cent upto graduate; and to 0.05 per cent upto post-graduate level. The illiterates are found to be as high as 56.57 per cent.

2. *Urban Areas*

The educational level of minority population in urban areas has been recorded in table II.5. In Rampur city, 24.19 per cent of minority population are found educated upto primary level; 10.42 per cent upto junior high school; 6.59 per cent upto high school; 2.87 per cent upto intermediate; 2.16 per cent upto graduate; and to 0.60 per cent upto post-graduate level. The illiterate population comes to 53.17 per cent. In Swar city, 47.26 per cent of minority population are found educated upto primary level; 6.47 per cent upto junior high school; and to 0.50 per cent upto high school. The illiterate population is found to be 45.77 per cent.

In these two cities (Rampur and Swar), 28.67 per cent of minority population are found educated upto primary; 9.65 per cent upto junior high school; 5.40 per cent upto high school; 2.32 per cent upto intermediate; 1.74 per cent upto graduate; and to 0.48 per cent upto post-graduate level. The illiterate minority population is found to be 51.74 per cent. Thus, a majority of population from minorities has obtained education mainly upto primary level. Illiteracy has, thus, prevailed in these two cities, but it is relatively more intense in Rampur (53.17 per cent) than to that in Swar (45.77 per cent).

In rural and urban total, 30.70 per cent of minority population has acquired education upto primary level; 7.61 per cent upto junior high school; 4.25 per cent upto high school; 1.41 per cent upto intermediate; 0.94 per cent upto graduate; and to 0.20 per cent upto post-graduate level. The illiterates are found to be as high as 54.89 per cent (Table II.5). This suggests that a majority of minority

TABLE II.5

Block-wise Level of Education of Minorities in Rural and Urban Areas : Rampur, 1997

Area	*Level of education upto:*								
	Primary (No.)	*Junior high school (No.)*	*High school (No.)*	*Inter-mediate (No.)*	*Graduate (No.)*	*Post-Graduate (No.)*	*Techni-cal / Diploma*	*Illiterate (No.)*	*Total (No.)*
A. Rural Blocks									
Bilaspur	196(22.82)	73(8.50)	43(5.00)	15(1.75)	9(1.05)	1(0.11)	- -	522(60.77)	859(100.0)
Swar	423(38.84)	54(4.96)	28(2.57)	3(0.28)	1(0.09)	- -	- -	580(53.26)	1089(100.0)
Sub-Total	**619(31.78)**	**127(6.52)**	**71(3.65)**	**18(0.92)**	**10(0.51)**	**1(0.05)**	**- -**	**1102(56.57)**	**1948(100.0)**
B. Urban Cities									
Rampur	202(24.19)	87(10.42)	55(6.59)	24(2.87)	18(2.16)	5(0.60)	- -	444(53.17)	835(100.0)
Swar	95(47.26)	13(6.47)	1(0.50)	- -	- -	- -	- -	92(45.77)	201(100.0)
Sub-Total	**297(28.67)**	**100(9.65)**	**56(5.40)**	**24(2.32)**	**18(1.74)**	**5(0.48)**	**- -**	**536(51.74)**	**1036(100.0)**
Grand Total	**916(30.70)**	**227(7.61)**	**127(4.25)**	**42(1.41)**	**28(0.94)**	**6(0.20)**	**- -**	**1638(54.89)**	**2984(100.0)**

Note: Figures in the bracket show per cent to total minority population.

Source: Based on the information collected from the field.

population is either illiterate or their level of education is mainly confined upto primary standard.

3. Enrolment, Non-Enrolment and Drop-Outs in Minorities

3.1 Rural Areas

Tables II.6, II.7 and II.8 portray age-wise enrolment, non-enrolment and drop-out for minority males and females in Bilaspur block. It is found that with the increase of age, the enrolment of males declines. For instance, the enrolment of males, which was 71.09 per cent in the age group of 6-11 years drastically declined to 58.97 per cent in the age group of 11-14 years and to 22.79 per cent in the age group

TABLE II.6

Enrolment, Non-Enrolment and Drop-Outs Across Age and Sex in Bilaspur Block in Rural Areas: Rampur, 1997

Block / Sex	*Age group*	*Minority children in family (No.)*	*Never enrolled (No.)*	*Drop out (No.)*	*Enrolled (No.)*
Bilaspur					
	06-11	83(100.00)	23(27.71)	1(1.20)	59(71.09)
Male	11-14	39(100.00)	11(28.20)	5(12.83)	23(58.97)
	15-20	79(100.00)	28(35.44)	33(41.77)	18(22.79)
Sub-Total		**201(100.0)**	**62(30.85)**	**39(19.40)**	**100(49.75)**
	06-11	57(100.00)	30(52.63)	2(3.51)	25(43.86)
Female	11-14	27(100.00)	19(70.37)	2(7.40)	6(22.23)
	15-20	47(100.00)	26(55.32)	10(21.28)	11(23.40)
Sub-Total		**131(100.0)**	**75(57.25)**	**14(10.69)**	**42(32.06)**
	06-11	140(100.00)	53(37.86)	3(2.14)	84(60.00)
Total	11-14	66(100.00)	35(45.45)	7(10.16)	29(43.94)
	15-20	126(100.00)	54(42.86)	43(34.13)	29(23.01)
Grand Total		**332(100.00)**	**137(41.26)**	**53(15.96)**	**142(42.78)**

Note: Figures under bracket indicate percent to children in different age groups, sub-total and total belonging to minority community.

Source: Based on the information collected from the field.

of 15-20 years. Such a decline in enrolment of males was accompanied by the rise in their drop-outs and non-enrolment. In Bilaspur block, of the total minority male children in all age groups, 49.75 per cent of males, are found enrolled, 19.40 per cent were drop outs and to 30.85 per cent are found never enrolled themselves for education (Table II.6).

As for the enrolment of females, 43.86 per cent were enrolled in the age group of 6-11 years, which declined to 22.23 per cent in the age group of 11-14 years. However, after this age group, the enrolment of females in the age group of 15-20 years increased to 23.40 per cent. Such a pattern of enrolment was accompanied with non-enrolment, which moved up from 52.63 per cent in the age group of 6-11 years to 70.37 per cent in the age group of 11-14 years. It declined at 55.32 per cent in the age group of 15-20 years. In Bilaspur block, of the total female minority children in all age groups, 32.06 per cent are found enrolled, 57.25 per cent never-enrolled and to 10.69 per cent are found drop outs (Table II.6). In Bilaspur block, the enrolment (males and females) decreased, drop outs increased and to that of never-enrolled fluctuated. In all age groups, enrolment (males and females) comes to be 42.78 per cent, never-enrolled 41.26 per cent and that of drop outs to 15.96 per cent.

Such a finding is also found consistent, to a large extent, in the case of Swar block as well. If we move from lower age group to higher age group, the enrolment of children declines, while there is an increase in non-enrolment and drop outs increase simultaneously. This is found true both for males and females. In Swar block, the enrolment of males in all age groups is found to 63.60 per cent, non-enrolment 25.17 per cent and to that of dropouts to 11.23 per cent, while for females to 48.20 per cent, 44.62 per cent and to 7.18 per cent respectively (Table II.7). In this block, the enrolment of minority children (males and females)

TABLE II.7

Enrolment, Non-Enrolment and Drop-Outs Across Age and Sex in Swar Block in Rural Areas: Rampur, 1997

Block / Sex	*Age group*	*Minority children in family (No.)*	*Never enrolled (No.)*	*Drop out (No.)*	*Enrolled (No.)*
Bilaspur					
	06-11	154 (100.00)	14(9.09)	1(0.65)	139(90.26)
Male	11-14	52(100.00)	12(23.08)	2(3.85)	38(73.07)
	15-20	88(100.00)	48(54.55)	30(34.09)	10(11.36)
Sub-Total		**294(100.0)**	**74(25.17)**	**33(11.23)**	**187(63.60)**
	06-11	105(100.00)	26(24.76)	1(0.95)	78(74.29)
Female	11-14	51(100.00)	30(58.82)	7(13.72)	14(27.45)
	15-20	39(100.00)	31(79.48)	6(15.38)	2(5.14)
Sub-Total		195(100.0)	87(44.62)	14(7.18)	94(48.20)
	06-11	259(100.00)	40(15.45)	2(0.77)	217(83.78)
Total	11-14	103(100.00)	42(40.78)	9(8.74)	52(50.48)
	15-20	127(100.00)	79(62.20)	36(28.35)	12(9.45)
Grand Total		489(100.00)	161(32.92)	47(9.61)	281(57.47)

Note: Figures within parentheses indicate percent to children in different age groups, sub-total and total belonging to minority community.

Source: Based on the information collected from the field.

was found to be 57.47 per cent, non-enrolment to 32.92 per cent and to that of drop out to 9.61 per cent. Thus, in Swar block also the enrolment declined, while non-enrolment and drop-outs increased from low age group to higher age group. In rural areas total, the enrolment of males and females declined, whereas, non-enrolment and drop-outs increased simultaneously from low age profile to high age profile (Table II.8).

Table II.9 gives the age-wise enrolment of males and females by educational institutions in Bilaspur block. It is found that 67.00 per cent of male students have been enrolled in government schools, 24 per cent in private schools and remaining 9 per cent in madarasas. The corres-

TABLE II.8

Enrolment, Non-Enrolment and Drop-Outs Across Age and Sex in Rural Areas : Rampur, 1997

Block/Sex	*Age group*	*Minority children in family (No.)*	*Never enrolled (No.)*	*Drop out (No.)*	*Enrolled (No.)*
		Bilaspur			
	06-11	237(100.00)	37(15.61)	2(0.84)	198(83.54)
Rural Male	11-14	91(100.00)	23(25.27)	7(7.69)	61(67.03)
	15-20	167(100.00)	76(45.51)	63(37.72)	28(16.77)
Sub-Total		**495(100.00)**	**136(27.47)**	**72(14.55)**	**287(57.98)**
	06-11	162(100.00)	56(34.57)	3(1.85)	103(63.58)
Rural Female	11-14	78(100.00)	49(62.82)	9(11.54)	20(25.64)
	15-20	86(100.00)	57(66.28)	16(18.60)	13(15.12)
Sub-Total		**326(100.00)**	**162(49.69)**	**28(8.59)**	**136(41.72)**
	06-11	399(100.00)	93(23.31)	5(1.25)	301(75.44)
Total	11-14	169(100.00)	72(42.60)	16(9.47)	81(47.93)
	15-20	253(100.00)	133(52.57)	79(31.23)	41(16.20)
Grand Total		821(100.00)	298(36.30)	100(12.18)	423(51.52)

Note: Figures within parentheses indicate percent to children of different age groups, sub-total and total belonging to minority community.

Source: Based on the information collected from the field.

ponding figures forfemales are found to be 57.15 per cent, 28.57 per cent and to 14.28 per cent respectively. In Bilaspur block, 64.08 per cent of minority children (males and females) are found enrolled in Government schools, 25.35 per cent in private schools and to 10.57 per cent in madarsas.

In Swar block, the enrolment of males is found to be 89.84 per cent in government schools, 2.67 per cent in private schools and to 7.49 per cent in madarasas. The enrolment for females is found to be 70.22 per cent in government schools, 8.51 per cent in private schools and to 21.27 per cent in madarsas. In Swar block, 83.27 per cent of minority children (males and females) are found enrolled in Government schools, 4.63 per cent in private schools and to 12.10 per cent in madarsas (Table II.10). In Bilaspur and Swar blocks together, 76.83 per cent of minority students (males and females) are found enrolled in government schools, 11.59 per cent in private schools and to 11.59 per cent in madarasas (Table II.11). It suggests that government and private schools are the primary centres of learning, yet madarasas have emerged as more important learning centres for females than to that of males for educational development.

TABLE II.9

Enrolment of Minority Students by Different Educational Institutions in Bilaspur Block in Rural Areas: Rampur, 1997

Block / Sex	*Age group*	*Educational institutions*			
		Govt. Schools (No.)	*Private Schools (No.)*	*Madarsas (No.)*	*Total*
		Bilaspur Block			
	06-11	41(69.49)	11(18.64)	7(11.87)	59(100.00)
Rural Male	11-14	12(52.17)	10(43.48)	1(4.35)	23(100.00)
	15-20	14(77.78)	3(16.67)	1(5.55)	18(100.00)
Sub-Total		**67(67.00)**	**24(24.00)**	**9(9.00)**	**100(100.00)**
	06-11	13(52.00)	7(28.00)	5(20.00)	25(100.00)
Rural Female	11-14	4(66.67)	1(17.66)	1(16.67)	6(100.00)
	15-20	7(63.64)	4(36.36)	--	11(100.00)
Sub-Total		**24(57.15)**	**12(28.57)**	**6(14.28)**	**42(100.00)**
	06-11	54(64.29)	18(21.43)	12(14.28)	84(100.00)
Total	11-14	16(55.17)	11(37.93)	2(6.90)	29(100.00)
	15-20	21(72.41)	7(24.14)	1(3.45)	29(100.00)
Grand Total		**91(64.08)**	**36(25.35)**	**15(10.57)**	**142(100.00)**

Note: Figures under bracket indicate percent to age-wise, sub-total and total children of the minority community.

Source: Based on the information collected from the field.

TABLE II.10

Enrolment of Minority Students by Different Educational Institutions in Swar Block in Rural Areas : Rampur,1997

Block / Sex	*Age group*	*Govt. Schools (No.)*	*Private Schools (No.)*	*Madarsas (No.)*	*Total*
		Educational institutions			
Swar Block					
	06-11	124(89.21)	2(1.44)	13(9.35)	139(100.00)
Rural Male	11-14	34(89.47)	3(7.89)	1(2.64)	38(100.00)
	15-20	10(100.0)	--	--	10(100.00)
Sub-Total		**168(89.84)**	**5(2.67)**	**14(7.49)**	**187(100.00)**
	06-11	53(67.95)	8(10.26)	17(21.79)	78(100.00)
Rural Female	11-14	12(85.72)	--	2(14.28)	14(100.00)
	15-20	1(50.00)	--	1(50.00)	2(100.00)
Sub-Total		**66(70.22)**	**8(8.51)**	**20(21.27)**	**94(100.00)**
	06-11	117(81.57)	10(4.61)	30(13.82)	217(100.00)
Total	11-14	46(88.46)	3(5.77)	3(5.77)	52(100.00)
	15-20	11(91.67)	--	1(8.33)	12(100.00)
Grand Total		**234(83.27)**	**13(4.63)**	**34(12.10)**	**281(100.00)**

Note: Figures under bracket indicate percent to age-wise, sub-total and total children of the minority community.

Source: Based on the information collected from the field.

3.2 Urban Areas

We may now discuss the enrolment, non-enrolment and drop outs in Rampur and Swar cities. In Rampur city, the enrolment of male and female declined in lower age group, whereas to that of non-enrolment increased from lower to higher age profile. In Rampur city, enrolled children (males and females) accounted for 57.69 per cent, never-enrolled 29.29 per cent and drop outs to 13.02 per cent (Table II.12). In Swar city, enrolment for males fluctuates, never-enrolled increased, while drop out was found to be constant in low to high age profile. Enrolment of females decreases, non-enrolment increased, while that of drop out declined when we moved from low age profile to high age profile (Table II.13). In urban total (Rampur and Swar cities), of the total minority children in all age groups, 61.03 per cent of minority children were found enrolled, 25.59 per cent never-enrolled, while to 13.38 per cent were the drop outs (Table II.14).

TABLE II.11

Enrolment of Minority Students by Different Educational Institutions in Rural Areas: Rampur, 1997

Block/Sex	*Age group*	*Educational institutions* *Govt. Schools (No.)*	*Private Schools (No.)*	*Madarsas (No.)*	*Total*
	06-11	165(83.33)	13(6.57)	20(10.10)	198(100.00)
Rural Male	11-14	46(75.41)	13(21.31)	2(3.28)	61(100.00)
	15-20	24(85.71)	3(10.72)	1(3.57)	28(100.00)
Sub-Total		**235(81.88)**	**29(10.11)**	**23(8.01)**	**287(100.00)**
	06-11	66(64.08)	15(14.56)	22(21.36)	103(100.00)
Rural Female	11-14	16(80.00)	1(5.00)	3(15.00)	20(100.00)
	15-20	8(61.54)	4(30.77)	1(7.69)	13(100.00)
Sub-Total		**90(66.18)**	**20(14.70)**	**26(19.12)**	**136(100.00)**
	06-11	231(76.75)	28(9.30)	42(13.95)	301(100.00)
Total	11-14	62(76.55)	14(17.28)	5(6.17)	81(100.00)
	15-20	32(78.04)	7(17.08)	2(4.88)	41(100.00)
Grand Total		**325(76.82)**	**49(11.59)**	**49(11.59)**	**423(100.00)**

Note: Figures within parentheses indicate percent to age-wise, sub-total and total children of the minority community.

Source: Based on the information collected from the field.

TABLE II.12

Enrolment, Non-Enrolment and Drop-Outs Across Age and Sex in Rampur City: Rampur, 1997

Block / Sex	*Age group*	*Minority children in family (No.)*	*Never enrolled (No.)*	*Drop out (No.)*	*Enrolled (No.)*
		Rampur City			
	06-11	74(100.00)	9(12.16)	1(1.35)	64(86.49)
Male	11-14	35(100.00)	7(20.00)	--	28(80.00)
	15-20	74(100.00)	28(37.84)	18(24.32)	28(37.84)
Sub-Total		**183(100.00)**	**44(24.04)**	**19(10.28)**	**120(65.58)**
	06-11	53(100.00)	12(22.64)	--	41(77.36)
Female	11-14	31(100.00)	12(38.71)	1(3.23)	18(58.06)
	15-20	71(100.00)	31(43.66)	24(33.80)	16(22.54)
Sub-Total		**155(100.00)**	**55(35.48)**	**25(16.13)**	**75(48.39)**
	06-11	127(100.00)	21(16.53)	1(0.79)	105(82.68)
Total	11-14	66(100.00)	19(28.79)	1(1.51)	46(69.70)
	15-20	145(100.00)	59(40.69)	42(28.97)	44(30.34)
Grand Total		**338(100.00)**	**99(29.29)**	**44(13.02)**	**195(57.69)**

Note: Figures within parentheses indicate percent to children in different age groups, sub-total and total belonging to minority community.

Source: Based on the information collected from the field.

TABLE II.13

Enrolment, Non-Enrolment and Drop-Outs Across Age and Sex in Swar City: Rampur, 1997

Block / Sex	*Age group*	*Minority children in family (No.)*	*Never enrolled (No.)*	*Drop out (No.)*	*Enrolled (No.)*
		Swarr City			
	06-11	24(100.00)	--	--	24(100.0)
Male	11-14	4(100.00)	1(25.00)	1(25.00)	2(50.00)
	15-20	7(100.00)	2(28.57)	1(14.29)	4(57.14)
Sub-Total		**35(100.00)**	**3(8.58)**	**2(5.71)**	**30(85.71)**
	06-11	29(100.00)	1(3.45)	--	28(96.55)
Female	11-14	14(100.00)	1(7.14)	6(42.86)	7(50.00)
	15-20	10(100.00)	5(50.00)	5(50.00)	--
Sub-Total		**53(100.00)**	**7(13.21)**	**11(20.75)**	**35(66.04)**

	06-11	53(100.00)	1(1.89)	--	52(98.11)
Total	11-14	18(100.00)	2(11.11)	7(38.89)	9(50.00)
	15-20	17(100.00)	7(41.18)	6(35.29)	4(23.53)
Grand Total		**88(100.00)**	**10(11.36)**	**13(14.77)**	**65(73.86)**

Note: Figures within parentheses indicate percent to children in different age groups, sub-total and total belonging to minority community.

Source: Based on the information collected from the field.

TABLE II.14

Enrolment, Non-Enrolment and Drop-Outs Across Age and Sex in Urban Areas: Rampur, 1997

Cities / Sex	*Age group*	*Minority children in family (No.)*	*Never enrolled (No.)*	*Drop out (No.)*	*Enrolled (No.)*
	06-11	98(100.00)	9(9.18)	1(1.02)	88(89.79)
Urban Male	11-14	39(100.00)	8(20.561)	1(2.56)	30(76.92)
	15-20	81(100.00)	30(37.04)	19(23.46)	32(39.51)
Sub-Total		**218(100.00)**	**47(21.56)**	**21(9.63)**	**150(68.81)**
	06-11	82(100.00)	13(15.85)	--	69(84.15)
Urban Female	11-14	45(100.00)	13(28.89)	7(15.55)	25(55.55)
	15-20	81(100.00)	36(44.44)	29(35.80)	16(19.75)
Sub-Total		**208(100.00)**	**62(29.81)**	**36(17.71)**	**110(52.88)**
	06-11	180(100.00)	22(12.22)	1(0.55)	157(87.23)
Total	11-14	84(100.00)	21(25.00)	8(9.52)	55(65.48)
	15-20	162(100.00)	66(40.74)	48(29.63)	48(29.63)
Grand Total		**426(100.00)**	**109(25.59)**	**57(13.38)**	**260(61.03)**

Note: Figures within parentheses indicate percent to children in different age groups, sub-total and total belonging to minority community.

Source: Based on the information collected from the field.

Tables II.15 and II.16 exhibit the enrolment by different educational institutions. Government schools and private schools have occupied the top position, where majority of males and females are found enrolled. Madarasa as educational institution is found at the bottom. In Rampur and Swar cities, as high as 56.92 per cent of students form minority community have been found enrolled in government schools, 33.46 per cent in private schools, while to 9.62 per cent in Madarasas.

TABLE II.15

Enrolment of Minority Students in Different Educational Institutions Across Age-Groups and Sex in Rampur District, 1997

Block / Sex	*Age group*	*Educational institutions* Govt. Schools (No.)	*Private Schools (No.)*	*Madarsas (No.)*	*Total*
		Rampur City			
	06-11	26(40.63)	34(53.13)	4(6.24)	64(100.00)
Male	11-14	15(53.57)	12(42.86)	1(3.57)	28(100.00)
	15-20	25(89.29)	3(10.71)	--	28(100.00)
Sub-Total		**66(55.00)**	**49(40.83)**	**5(4.17)**	**120(100.00)**
	06-11	17(41.46)	22(53.66)	2(4.88)	41(100.00)
Female	11-14	13(72.22)	5(27.78)	--	18(100.00)
	15-20	11(68.75)	1(6.25)	4(25.00)	16(100.00)
Sub-Total		**41(54.67)**	**28(37.33)**	**6(8.00)**	**75(100.00)**
	06-11	43(40.95)	56(53.33)	6(5.72)	105(100.00)
	11-14	28(60.96)	17(36.98)	1(2.16)	46(100.00)
	15-20	36(81.82)	4(9.09)	4(98.09)	44(100.00)
Grand Total		**107(54.87)**	**77(39.49)**	**11(5.64)**	**195(100.00)**

Note: Figures within parentheses indicate per cent to age-wise, sub-total and total children of the minority community.

Source: Based on the information collected from the field.

In rural and urban total, of the minority children in all age-groups, 54.77 per cent are found enrolled, 32.64 per cent never enrolled, while to 12.59 per cent are drop-outs. Enrolled students are highest in the age group of 6 to 11 years (79.10 per cent) and that of drop-outs (30.60

per cent) in age-groups of 15 to 20 years. This is found true for males as well as females (Table II.18). Also, a majority of enrolled students in rural and urban areas, is found enrolled in government schools (69.25 per cent), in private schools (19.91 per cent) and in Madarasas (10.84 per cent). This is portrayed in Table II.19.

TABLE II.16

Enrolment of Minority Students in Different Educational Institutions Across Age-Groups and Sex in Swar District, 1997

Block / Sex	*Age group*	*Educational institutions*			
		Govt. Schools (No.)	*Private Schools (No.)*	*Madarsas (No.)*	*Total*
		Swar Block			
	06-11	15(62.50)	8(33.33)	1(4.17)	24(100.00)
Male	11-14	2(100.0)	--	--	2(100.00)
	15-20	4(100.0)	--	--	4(100.00)
Sub-Total		**21(70.00)**	**8(26.67)**	**1(3.33)**	**30(100.00)**
	06-11	16(57.14)	1(3.57)	11(39.29)	28(100.00)
Female	11-14	4(57.14)	1(14.29)	2(28.57)	7(100.00)
	15-20	--	--	--	--
Sub-Total		**20(57.15)**	**2(5.71)**	**13(37.14)**	**35(100.00)**
	06-11	31(59.61)	9(13.31)	12(23.08)	52(100.00)
Total	11-14	6(66.67)	1(11.11)	2(22.22)	9(100.00)
	15-20	4(100.0)	--	--	4(100.00)
Grand Total		**41(63.08)**	**10(15.38)**	**14(21.54)**	**65(100.00)**

Note: Figures under bracket indicate per cent to age-wise, sub-total and total children of the minority community.

Source: Based on the information collected from the field.

TABLE II.17

Enrolment of Minority Students in Different Educational Institutions Across Age-Groups and Sex in Urban Areas: Rampur, 1997

Block / Sex	*Age group*	*Educational institutions*			
		Govt. Schools (No.)	*Private Schools (No.)*	*Madarsas (No.)*	*Total*
	06-11	41(46.59)	42(47.73)	5(5.68)	88(100.00)
Urban Male	11-14	17(56.67)	12(40.00)	1(3.33)	30(100.00)
	15-20	29(90.63)	3(9.37)	--	32(100.00)
Sub-Total		**87(58.00)**	**57(38.00)**	**6(4.00)**	**150(100.00)**
	06-11	33(47.83)	23(33.33)	13(18.84)	69(100.00)
Urban Female	11-14	17(68.00)	6(24.00)	2(8.00)	25(100.00)
	15-20	11(68.75)	1(6.25)	4(25.00)	16(100.00)
Sub-Total		**61(55.46)**	**30(27.27)**	**19(17.27)**	**110(100.00)**
	06-11	74(47.13)	65(41.40)	18(11.47)	157(100.00)
Total	11-14	34(61.82)	18(32.73)	3(5.45)	55(100.00)
	15-20	40(83.34)	4(8.33)	4(8.33)	48(100.00)
Grand Total		**148(56.92)**	**87(33.46)**	**25(9.62)**	**260(100.00)**

Note: Figures under bracket indicate per cent to age-wise, sub-total and total children of the minority community.

Source: Based on the information collected from the field.

TABLE II.18

Enrolment, Non-Enrolment and Drop-Outs of Minority Children in Rural and Urban Areas by Age and Sex: Rampur, 1997

Block/Sex	*Age group*	*Minority children in family (No.)*	*Never enrolled (No.)*	*Drop out (No.)*	*Enrolled (No.)*
		Rampur City			
	06-11	335(100.00)	46(13.73)	3(0.90)	286(85.37)
Male	11-14	130(100.00)	31(23.85)	8(6.15)	91(70.00)
	15-20	248(100.00)	106(42.74)	82(33.07)	60(24.19)
Sub-Total		**713(100.00)**	**183(25.67)**	**93(13.04)**	**437(61.29)**
	06-11	244(100.00)	69(28.28)	3(1.23)	172(70.49)
Female	11-14	123(100.00)	62(50.41)	16(13.01)	45(36.58)
	15-20	167(100.00)	93(55.69)	45(26.95)	29(17.36)
Sub-Total		**534(100.00)**	**224(41.95)**	**64(11.98)**	**246(46.07)**
	06-11	579(100.00)	115(19.86)	6(1.04)	458(79.10)
Total	11-14	253(100.00)	93(36.76)	24(9.49)	136(53.75)
	15-20	415(100.00)	199(47.95)	127(30.60)	89(21.45)
Grand Total		**1247(100.00)**	**407(32.64)**	**157(12.59)**	**683(54.77)**

Note: Figures within parentheses indicate percent to age-wise, sub-total and total children of the to minority community.

Source: Based on the information collected from the field.

Secondary information collected from BSA/DIOS by the Department of District Minority Welfare from the Rampur has also been recorded in Table II.20. In district Rampur, out of 1020 schools, there are 860 junior basic schools (or 84.31 per cent); 11 senior basic schools (or 11.08 per cent); 25 high schools (or 2.45 per cent); and to 22 intermediate colleges (or 2.16 per cent). Further, out of 416 educational institutions with Urdu teachers, junior basic schools are 325 (or 78.13 per cent); senior basic schools 75 (or 18.03 per cent); high schools 12 (or 2.88 per cent); and intermediate colleges 4 (or 0.96 per cent) in the Rampur district.

TABLE II.19

Enrolment of Minority Students in Different Educational Institutions Across Age-Groups and Sex in Urban Areas: Rampur, 1997

Block / Sex	*Age group*	*Educational institutions*			
		Govt. Schools (No.)	*Private Schools (No.)*	*Madarsas (No.)*	*Total*
	06-11	206(72.03)	55(19.23)	25(8.74)	286(100.00)
Urban Male	11-14	63(69.23)	25(27.47)	3(3.30)	91(100.00)
	15-20	53(88.33)	6(10.00)	1(1.67)	60(100.00)
Sub-Total		**322(73.68)**	**86(19.68)**	**29(6.64)**	**437(100.00)**
	06-11	99(57.56)	38(22.09)	35(20.35)	172(100.00)
Urban Female	11-14	33(73.33)	7(15.56)	5(11.11)	45(100.00)
	15-20	19(65.52)	5(17.24)	5(17.24)	29(100.00)
Sub-Total		**151(61.38)**	**50(20.33)**	**45(18.29)**	**246(100.00)**
	06-11	305(66.59)	93(20.31)	60(13.10)	458(100.00)
Total	11-14	96(70.59)	32(23.53)	8(5.88)	136(100.00)
	15-20	72(80.90)	11(12.36)	6(6.74)	89(100.00)
Grand Total		**473(69.25)**	**136(19.91)**	**74(10.84)**	**683(100.00)**

Note: Figures within parentheses indicate per cent to age-wise, sub-total and total children of the minority community.

Source: Based on the information collected from the field.

TABLE II.20

Educational Institutions and Enrolment of Minority Male and Female Students in Rampur District, 1997

Particulars	*Junior basic schools*	*Senior basic schools*	*High schools*	*Intermediate colleges*	*Total*
Schools (No.)	860(84.31)	113(11.08)	25(2.45)	22(2.16)	1020(100.0)
Schools with Urdu teachers (No.)	325(78.13)	75(18.03)	12(2.88)	4(0.96)	416(100.00)
Minority boys enrolled (No.)	24041(70.54)	1328(3.90)	7257(21.29)	1456(4.27)	34082(100.0)
Minority girls enrolled (No.)	12581(75.86)	1550(9.35)	1848(11.14)	605(3.65)	16584(100.0)

Note: Figures within parentheses denote per cent to horizontal total.

Source: BSA/DIOS, Rampur, 1997.

The number of minority male students enrolled in junior basic schools is found to be the highest, i.e. 24,041 (or 70.54 per cent) followed by in high schools, i.e., 7,257 (or 21.29 per cent). The corresponding figures come to 1,328 (or 3.90 per cent) in senior basic schools and 1,456 (or 4.27 per cent) in intermediate colleges. A much similar is also the case for minority females enrolled in different schools. It is found that 12,581 (or 75.86 per cent) minority girls are found enrolled in junior basic schools; and to 1,848 (or 11.14 per cent) in high schools. The respective figures are found to be 1,550 (or 9.35 per cent) in senior basic schools and 605 (or 3.65 per cent) in intermediate colleges. Thus, number of schools with Urdu teachers and minority male and female students have generally declined from lower to higher level of educational institutions.

Information has also been collected from District Minority Welfare Officer, Rampur on madarsas, teachers and enrolment of minority students across different levels of education. This is recorded in Table II.21. Total number of madarsas is found to be 101, of which 49 (or 48.52 per cent) belong to Tahtania (junior basic school, i.e. upto primary level); 40 (or 39.60 per cent) Faucania (senior basic schools, i.e. from class VI to VIII); 5 (or 4.95 per cent) Munshi/Maulvi (i.e. upto high school); 4 (or 3.96 per cent) Alim (or upto Intermediate level); and 3 (or 2.97 per cent) Kamil/Fazil (or upto Graduate/Post graduate levels). Recognized madarsas are found to be 2 at each level of education, while unrecognized madarsas 14 each for Tahtania and Faucania. The number of teachers in recognized madarsas has been found to be 15, which have gradually declined from lower to higher level of educational institutions. The same is also the case for teachers in unrecognized madarsas. The number of teachers in unrecognized madarsas is found to be 48, which have declined gradually from 28 in Tahtania to 20 in Faucania.

As for the enrolment of boys and girls, it has gradually

TABLE II.21

Madarasas, Teachers and Enrolment at Various Levels of Education in Rampur, 1997

Particulars	Level of education					
	Tahtania	*Faucania*	*Munshi/ Maulvi*	*Alim*	*Kamil/ Fazil*	*Total*
Recognized madarasas (No.)	2(20.00)	2(20.00)	2(20.00)	2(20.00)	2(20.00)	10(100.0)
Unrecognised madarasas (No.)	14(50.00)	14(50.00)	- -	- -	- -	28(100.00)
Recognised teachers (No.)	5(33.33)	4(26.67)	3(20.00)	2(13.33)	1(6.67)	15(100.00)
Unrecognized teachers (No.)	28(58.33)	20(41.67)	- -	- -	- -	48(100.00)
Total madarasas (No.)	49(48.52)	40(39.60)	5(4.95)	4(3.96)	3(2.97)	101(100.00)
Enrolment of boys (No.)	23425(37.49)	20201(32.33)	16000(25.60)	2000(3.20)	860(1.38)	62486(100.0)
Enrolment of girls (No.)	13402(80.38)	32.72(19.62)	- -	- -	- -	16674(100.0)
Total enrolment of boys and girls (No.)	36827(46.52)	23473(29.66)	16000(20.21)	2000(2.52)	860(1.09)	79160(100.0)

reduced from lower to higher level of educational institutions. For example, of the total enrolment of boys (62,486), the enrolment of boys declined from 37.49 per cent in Tahtania to 32.33 per cent in Faucania; from 25.60 per cent in Munshi/Maulvi; to 3.20 per cent in Alim and to 1.38 per cent in Kamil/Fazil. Similarly, of the total enrolment of girls (16,674), the enrolment of girls has reduced drastically from 80.38 per cent in Tahtania to 19.62 per cent in Faucania (Table II.21). Thus, the above analysis suggests that total number of madarsas, teachers and enrolment of minority male and female students have declined gradually from lower to higher level of educational institutions (Table II.21).

3.3 Drop-outs in Rural and Urban Areas

We may now discuss the drop-outs across different levels of education of minority male and female students.

TABLE II.22

Class-wise Drop-outs of Minority Male and Female Students in Rural Areas: Rampur, 1997

Class	*Male (No.)*	*Female (No.)*	*Total (No.)*
First	4 (5.56)	1 (3.57)	5 (5.00)
Second	7 (9.72)	6 (21.43)	13 (13.00)
Third	3 (4.17)	2 (7.14)	5 (5.00)
Fourth	7 (9.72)	2 (7.14)	9 (9.00)
Fifth	24 (33.34)	10 (35.71)	34 (34.00)
Sixth	5 (6.94)	1 (3.57)	6 (6.00)
Seventh	2 (2.78)	--	2 (2.00)
Eighth	7 (9.72)	2 (7.14)	9 (9.00)
Ninth	5 (6.94)	--	5 (5.00)
Tenth	7 (9.72)	4 (14.20)	11 (11.00)
Eleventh	1 (1.39)	--	1 (1.00)
Twelfth	--	--	--
Total	72(100.0)	28(100.0)	100(100.00)

Note: Figures within parentheses denote per cent to vertical total.

Source: Based on the information collected from the field.

This is recorded in Table II.22 in case of rural areas. In rural areas, 33.34 per cent of male students from minority community have dropped out after class Vth; 9.72 per cent after Classes IInd, IVth, VIIIth and Xth and 6.94 per cent after classes VIth and IXth. Among the females, the highest drop outs are found to be after Class Vth (35.71 per cent), IInd (21.43 per cent), IIIrd, IVth and VIIIth (7.14 per cent each), etc. In rural areas total, minority students (males and females) have dropped out after Vth standard of education (34 per cent) followed by IInd (13 per cent). Drop out is found lowest after XIth standard of education (1 per cent).

TABLE II.23

Class-wise Drop-outs of Minority Male and Female Students in Urban Areas : Rampur, 1997

Class	*Male (No.)*	*Female (No.)*	*Total (No.)*
First	4 (5.56)	1 (3.57)	5 (5.00)
First	--	--	--
Second	1 (4.76)	1 (2.78)	2 (3.51)
Third	2 (9.52)	6 (16.66)	8 (14.03)
Fourth	2 (9.52)	7 (19.44)	9 (15.79)
Fifth	5 (23.81)	14 (38.89)	19 (33.33)
Sixth	--	1 (2.78)	1 (1.75)
Seventh	--	--	--
Eighth	3 (14.29)	1 (2.78)	4 (7.02)
Ninth	2 (9.52)	--	2 (3.51)
Tenth	4 (19.06)	2 (5.56)	6 (10.53)
Eleventh	--	--	--
Twelfth	2 (9.52)	4 (11.11)	6 (10.53)
Total	21(100.0)	36(100.0)	57(100.00)

Note: Figures within parentheses denote per cent to vertical total.
Source: Based on the information collected from the field.

Table II.23 presents dropouts for minority male and female students in urban areas. The drop outs of minority male students are found highest after Vth standard (23.81 per cent) followed by Xth (19.06 per cent), while it is found to be lowest after IInd standard (4.76 per cent). Dropouts for minority female students are found highest after V^{th} standard of education (38.89 per cent) followed by IVth (19.44 per cent), while it is lowest after IInd, VIth and VIIIth standards of education being to 2.78 per cent in each cases. In urban areas total, a majority of minority male and female students has dropped out after Vth standard (33.33 per cent). However, drop outs are found to be lowest after standard VIth (1.75 per cent).

TABLE II.24

Class-wise Drop-outs of Minority Male and Female Students in Rural and Urban Areas: Rampur, 1997

Class	*Male (No.)*	*Female (No.)*	*Total (No.)*
First	4 (4.30)	1 (1.56)	5 (3.18)
Second	8 (8.60)	7 (10.94)	15 (9.55)
Third	5 (5.38)	8 (12.50)	13 (8.28)
Fourth	9 (9.68)	9 (14.06)	18 (11.47)
Fifth	29 (31.18)	24 (37.50)	53 (33.76)
Sixth	5 (5.38)	2 (3.12)	7 (4.46)
Seventh	2 (2.15)	--	2 (1.27)
Eighth	10 (10.75)	3 (4.69)	13 (8.28)
Ninth	7 (7.53)	--	7 (4.46)
Tenth	11 (11.83)	6 (9.38)	17 (10.83)
Eleventh	1 (1.07)	--	1 (0.64)
Twelfth	2 (2.15)	4 (6.25)	6 (3.82)
Total	93 (100.0)	64 (100.0)	157 (100.00)

Note: Figures within parentheses denote percentage to vertical total.

Source: Based on the information collected from the field.

In Rampur district (rural and urban), a majority of minority male and female students has dropped out after V^{th} standard. It comes to 31.18 per cent for minority male students and to 37.50 per cent for minority female students. However, drop out for minority male students is found lowest after XIth standard (1.07 per cent), while that for female students after Ist standard of education (1.56 per cent). Taking male and female in rural and urban areas, a majority of minority students has dropped out after V^{th} standard (33.76 per cent), while drop outs are found to be lowest after XIth standard of education (0.64 per cent). Thus, a majority of minority students has dropped out after Vth standard of education (Table II.24).

3.4 Reasons for Low Level of Enrolment

We also traced from the minority respondents about the low enrolment of their children. The impressions from them have been recorded in Table II.25 across rural and urban areas. In rural areas, 288 (or 88.34 per cent) of minority respondents feel that enrolment of their children is low, while for 38 (or 11.66 per cent) it is not so. In urban areas, the corresponding figures come to 84.48 per cent and to 15.52 per cent respectively. In rural and urban total, 435 respondents (or 87 per cent) feel that enrolment of minority students is low, while for 65 (or 13 per cent) it is not so (Table II.25). Thus, enrolment of minority students has been reported to be generally low in Rampur district.

TABLE II.25

Responses of Respondents About the Enrolment of Minority Students in Rural and Urban Areas: Rampur, 1997

Rampur	*Responses of minority respondents about the low level of enrolment for minority students*		
	Yes (No.)	*No (No.)*	*Total (No.)*
Rural	288 (88.34)	38 (11.66)	326 (100.00)
Urban	147 (84.48)	27 (15.52)	174 (100.00)
Total	435 (87.00)	65 (13.00)	500 (100.00)

Note: Figures within parentheses denote per cent to total respondents.
Source: Based on the information collected from the field.

To investigate as to why the enrolment of minority

students is low, we have also enquired reasons from the minority respondents. A summary view of the responses of minority respondents has been recorded in Table II.26. A majority of respondents in rural areas (74.30 per cent) has expressed the poor economic conditions of parents as the main reason for the low level of enrolment. Next to this comes the studying of *Quran* and theology. This is particularly true for girls as 35.42 per cent of respondents have given weightage to it. Also, 29.86 per cent of minority respondents feel that long distance from home to school is a reason for low level of enrolment of minority students.

TABLE II.26

Reasons* Articulated by Minority Respondents for the Low Level of Enrolment of Minority Students in Rural and Urban Areas: Rampur, 1997

Reasons	*Rural (No.)*	*Urban (No.)*	*Total (No.)*
Poor economic conditions of parents	214(74.30)	103(70.07)	317(72.87)
No immediate returns of school education	64(22.22)	33(22.45)	97(22.30)
Poor job prospect after education	63(21.88)	44(29.93)	107(24.59)
Engagement of students in household work	72(25.00)	61(41.50)	133(30.57)
Ignorance of parents about the importance of education	52(18.05)	25(17.01)	77(17.70)
Insincere teachers in school	38(13.19)	29(19.73)	67(15.40)
School has no attraction due to its poor conditions	47(16.32)	36(24.48)	83(19.08)
Lack of interest among children	42(14.58)	24(16.33)	66(15.17)
School education not useful for girls	47(16.32)	38(25.85)	85(19.54)
Due to co-educational system in school	27(9.37)	16(10.88)	43(9.88)
No facility of teaching Urdu in school	77(26.73)	48(32.65)	125(28.74)
Study of Quran and Theology is enough for girls	102(35.42)	48(32.65)	150(34.48)
School at a long distance	86(29.86)	1(0.22)	87(20.00)
Others	2(0.69)	--	2(0.46)
N =	288(100.0)	147(100.0)	435(100.0)

* Indicates multiple responses.

Note: Figures within parentheses denote per cent to total respondents who offered reasons.

Source: Based on the information collected from the field.

In urban areas, as much as 70.07 per cent of minority respondents have expressed the poor economic conditions of parents as important factor for the low enrolment of education for their children. Second, in order of importance, comes the lack of teaching of Urdu in the schools and consideration of study of Quran and theology as sufficient for girls as main reasons for low level of enrolment.

In rural and urban total, 72.87 per cent of minority respondents cited the poor economic conditions of parents as a principal reason for the low enrolment of education. Next to this comes the consideration of knowledge of Quran and theology. This is particularly true for the girls.

Concluding Observations

This chapter examines the various social characteristics of minority community in the rural, urban and in the Rampur district. A majority of households from the minority community belongs to general caste category in rural (78.83 per cent), urban (63.22 per cent) and in the district (73.40 per cent). Also a majority of population from minorities in rural, urban and in the district is found to lees than 15 years in the rural as well as the urban areas.

As for marital status, 37.97 per cent of males and to 48.08 per cent of females in rural areas are married. In urban areas, 34.62 per cent of males while to 38.37 per cent of females are married. In the district, 40.35 per cent of minority population (males and females) are married, while 57.04 per cent are unmarried. The general finding thus suggests that unmarried population is relatively more significant than to that of married population among the minority community in Rampur district. The size of household worked out to be 5.97 in the district, which consists of 5.98 in rural and to 5.95 in urban areas.

As for the educational level, 43.43 per cent of minority population in rural areas are found educated, while 56.57

per cent are illiterates. In urban areas, the respective figures come to 48.26 per cent and to 51.57 per cent respectively. Thus, literacy is found higher in urban than that in rural areas. Also, a significant population from minorities has obtained education upto primary level, i.e. 31.78 per cent in rural, 28.67 per cent in urban and to 30.70 per cent in the district.

In rural areas, enrolment is found to be 51.52 per cent, non-enrolment to 36.30 per cent, and drop out to 12.18 per cent. In urban areas, the corresponding figures come to 61.03 per cent, 25.59 per cent and to 13.38 per cent respectively. Also, enrolment of minority students generally has declined, whereas, drop out and non-enrolment have increased from low age to high age profile. Also, Government schools are found as an important centre for education to the minority students. Madarsa has been found as a main centre of education for minority female students.

Analysis on class-wise drop out suggests that a majority of minority students (male and females) has dropped out after Class Vth. It is found to be 34 per cent in rural, 33.33 per cent in urban and to 33.76 per cent in the district. A majority of minority respondents, i.e. 88.34 per cent in rural, 84.48 per cent in urban and to 87 per cent in the district feel that enrolment of minority children is low, which is determined mainly by the poor economic conditions of parents, lack of teaching facility of Urdu in schools, distance from residence to school, study of Quran and theology and engagement of students in other important household activities. These relate to social characteristics of minorities, the economic conditions of minorities have been discussed in the next Chapter III, of the present study.

3

Economic Characteristics of Minorities

Introduction

In this chapter an attempt has been made to examine empirically the various economic aspects of minorities, such as, (i) engagement of minority households in different economic activities; (ii) levels income of minority households; (iii) poverty profile of minority households; and (iv) linkage pattern. In view of analytical convenience the analysis in this chapter has been carried out across blocks, rural and urban areas.

Minority Households Engaged in Different Economic Occupations

Table III.1 classifies the minority households across different economic occupations. In Bilaspur block, of the total households (122), 75 (or 61.47 per cent) are found engaged in farming. Next, in order of importance, comes the wage earners, in which accounted for 30.33 per cent, of the minority households. In Swar block, the most important occupation is the wage earning, in which a majority of households (49.51 per cent) has been engaged. Next, in order of importance, is the farming, which employs the 42.65 per cent of minority households. Business/trade and service are, hcwever, found to be relatively less significant as an observer of minority households.

In Bilaspur and Swar blocks together, farming emerges as the most important occupation, which has employed to

49.69 per cent of minority households. Next, in order of importance, comes the wage earning, which employs to 42.33 per cent of minority households. The next economic occupation is business/trade followed by service. In business/trade, 5.83 per cent of minority households are engaged, while in service, 2.15 per cent of minority households are found employed.

In Rampur city, out of 132 minority households, 47 households (or 35.61 per cent) are engaged as wage earners; 44 households (or 33.33 per cent) in business/trade; 20 households (or 15.15 per cent) in service; 18 households (or 13.64 per cent) in manufacturing; and to only 3 households (or 2.27 per cent) in other occupations. Thus, wage earning and business/trade are found to be the main economic occupations in Rampur city. In Swar city, out of 42 minority households, 19 households (or 45.24 per cent) are engaged in self-employed services; 14 households (or 33.33 per cent) in business/trade; and to 8 households (or 19.05 per cent) are found engaged as wage earners. Thus, in Swar city, self-employed and business/trade are found as the important economic occupations.

In urban total, business/trade occupies the top position, which out of 174 minority households has employed to 58 households (or 33.33 per cent). Next to this comes the wage earnings, which accounts for 31.61 per cent of employment followed by self-employed services (22.42 per cent) and manufacturing (10.92 per cent). It suggests that business/trade, wage earnings, self-employed services and manufacturing are the principal economic occupations in urban areas, in which a majority of minority households is found employed.

In the district (rural and urban), a majority of minority households is engaged in wage earning (38.60 per cent); in farming (32.40 per cent); in business/trade (15.40 per cent); and in self-employed services (7.80 per cent). However,

TABLE III.1

Distribution of Minority Households in Different Economic Occupations in Rural and Urban Areas : Rampur, 1997

Occupations	Rural			Urban			Total		
	Bilaspur	*Swar*	*Total*	*Rampur*	*Swar*	*Total*	*Rural*	*Urban*	*Total*
Wage Earning	37(30.33)	101(49.51)	138(42.33)	47(35.61)	8(19.05)	55(31.61)	138(42.33)	55(31.61)	193(38.60)
Farming	75(61.47)	87(42.65)	162(49.69)	--	--	--	162(49.69)	--	162(32.40)
Business/Trade	5(4.10)	14(6.86)	19(5.83)	44(33.33)	14(33.33)	58(33.33)	19(5.83)	58(33.33)	77(15.40)
Service	5(4.10)	2(0.98)	7(2.15)	--	--	--	7(2.15)	--	7(1.40)
Manufacturing	--	--	--	18(13.64)	1(2.38)	19(10.92)	--	19(10.92)	19(3.80)
Self-Employed Services	--	--	--	20(15.15)	19(45.24)	39(22.42)	--	39(22.42)	39(7.80)
Others	--	--	--	3(2.27)	--	3(1.72)	--	3(1.72)	3(0.60)
Total	122(100.0)	204(100.0)	326(100.0)	132(100.0)	42(100.0)	174(100.0)	326(100.0)	174(100.0)	500(100.0)

Note: Figures under bracket denote per cent to vertical total.

Source: Based on the information collected from the field.

TABLE III.2

Distribution of Minority Population by Different Economic Occupations in Rural and Urban Areas: Rampur, 1997

Occupations	*Rural*		*Urban*		*Total*		
	Bilaspur	*Swar*	*Rampur*	*Swar*	*Rural*	*Urban*	*Total*
Agriculture	84(7.78)	136(12.49)	4 (0.48)	--	220(11.39)	4(0.38)	224(7.51)
Agricultural labour	77(8.96)	102(9.37)	--	--	179(9.19)	--	179(6.00)
Non-agricultural labour	27(3.14)	58(5.33)	5(0.60)	--	85(4.36)	5(0.48)	90(3.02)
Cattle and animal care	3(0.35)	1(0.09)	--	--	4(0.21)	--	4(0.13)
Business	16(1.86)	4(0.37)	49(5.87)	15(7.46)	20(1.03)	64(6.17)	84(2.81)
Self-employed	17(1.98)	12(1.10)	46(5.51)	14(6.96)	29(1.49)	60(5.79)	89(2.98)
Service	32(3.73)	3(0.27)	10(1.20)	--	35(1.80)	10(0.96)	45(1.51)
Artisan	8(0.93)	--	17(2.04)	--	8(0.41)	17(1.64)	25(0.84)
Skilled worker	15(1.75)	2(0.18)	126(15.09)	26(12.94)	17(0.87)	152(14.67)	169(5.66)
Student	147(17.11)	291(26.72)	202(24.19)	65(32.34)	438(22.48)	267(25.77)	705(23.63)
Household work	277(32.25)	318(29.20)	261(31.26)	64(31.84)	595(30.54)	325(31.37)	920(30.83)
Others	156(18.16)	162(14.88)	115(13.77)	17(8.46)	318(16.32)	132(12.74)	450(15.08)
Total	859(100.0)	1089(100.0)	835(100.00)	201(100.0)	1948(100.0)	1036(100.0)	2984(100.0)

Note: Figures within parentheses denote per cent to vertical total.

Source: Based on the information collected from the field.

other economic occupations, like, manufacturing and services in government and non-government organizations have been found to be of marginal significance (Table III.1).

1. Minority Population Across Different Economic Occupations

Table III.2 classifies minority population across different economic occupations. In Bilaspur block, a majority of minority population (32.25 per cent) is found employed in household works. Next, in order of importance, comes the (i) other economic occupation; and those employed as (ii) agricultural labour, and in (iii) agriculture, in which 18.16 per cent, 8.96 per cent and to 7.78 per cent of minority population are employed respectively. Minority population engaged as self-employed, in business/trade and in skilled activity are found to be 1.98 per cent, 1.86 per cent and to 1.75 per cent respectivcly. Thus, in Bilaspur block, household work and agriculture are found as important economic occupations.

In Swar block, minority population employed in household works comes to 29.20 per cent; cultivators 12.49 per cent; agricultural labour 9.37 per cent; and to non-agricultural labour to 5.33 per cent. Thus, a majority of minority population is found engaged in household works and in agriculture. The importance of business/trade, service and self-employed activity are found to be of marginal significance. In Bilasur and Swar blocks, household work, other occupations and agriculture have been found relatively more significant than the rest as employer of minority population.

In Rampur city, 31.26 per cent of minority population are found engaged in household work; 15.09 per cent as skilled workers; and to 13.77 per cent are found employed in other economic occupations. The remaining economic occupations are found to be of relatively less significant.

In Swar city, 31.84 per cent of minority population are found engaged in household work; 12.94 per cent as skilled workers; 8.46 per cent in other economic occupation; 7.46 per cent in business/trade; and to 6.96 per cent in self-employed economic occupation. Thus, household work, business and trade have been found as employment intensive occupation in Swar city.

In urban total, household work, skilled worker intensive occupation and other economic occupation have been found more important than the rest. In rural and urban total, household work, other economic occupation and agriculture have been found as important economic occupations. In fact, household work has occupied the top position, whereas, cattle and animal care is found at the bottom in Rampur district (Table III.2).

Income Generation from Different Source and Level of Poverty Among Minorities

1. Income Per Household and Per Capita

We may now discuss the level of income of the minority households. Table III.3 gives the information on number of households, family members, total income, average family income and income per capita. Income per household has been arrived dividing total household income by number of respective households. Similarly, per capita income is derived dividing total income by total minority household population.

In Bilaspur block, the average household income comes to Rs.16,729.51, while income per capita to Rs.2,376.02. In Swar block, per household income works out to be Rs.13,695.10, while income per capita to Rs.2,663.30. Per capita income is found higher in Swar than that in the Bilaspur, while income per household is found higher in Bilaspur than that in Swar. In rural total, income per household is worked out to be Rs.14,830.67, while income per capita to Rs.2,533.96. Per capita income in Swar block is also found higher than that in Bilaspur and in the rural area total. Similarly, income per household in Bilaspur has been found to be higher than that in Swar and that in rural areas as a whole.

In Rampur city, the average household income comes to Rs.14,628.79, while income per capita to Rs.2,312.57. In Swar city, income per household is found to Rs.13,019.05, while per capita to Rs.2,720.40. In urban areas, average household income comes to Rs.14,240.23, while income per capita to Rs.2,391.70. Thus, per capita income in Swar city is found higher than Rampur city as well as the total of urban areas. Average household income is found higher in Rampur than that in Swar and urban total. In the district, income per household is found to be Rs.14,625.20, while income per capita to Rs.2,483.90 (Table III.3).

TABLE III.3

Households, Household Members, Income Per Household and Per Capita in Blocks and Cities : Rampur, 1997

Area	*Total house-holds (No.)*	*Household members (No.)*	*Total income (Rs.)*	*Income per house-hold (Rs.)*	*Income per capita (Rs.)*
I. Blocks					
A. Bilaspur	122	859	2041000.00	16729.51	2376.02
B. Swar	204	1049	2793800.00	13695.10	2663.30
Rural Total (A+B)	**326**	**1908**	**4834800.00**	**14830.67**	**2533.96**
II. Cities					
C. Rampur	132	835	1931000.00	14628.79	2312.57
D. Swar	42	201	546800.00	13019.05	2720.40
Urban Total (C+D)	**174**	**1036**	**2477800.00**	**14240.23**	**2391.70**
District (Rural+Urban)	**500**	**2944**	**7312600.00**	**14625.00**	**2483.90**

Source: Based on the information collected from the field.

2. Generation of Income from Different Sources

Table III.4 gives the generation of income from different sources. In Bilaspur block, the main source of income is

TABLE III.4

Income Generation in Blocks and Cities through Various Sources: Rampur, 1997

Area	*Agriculture (Rs.)*	*Property (Rs.)*	*Milch cattle (Rs.)*	*Poultry birds (Rs.)*	*Business, service, artisanal work, etc.* (Rs.)*	*Others (Rs.)*	*Total income (Rs.)*
I. Blocks							
A. Bilaspur	1010000.00 (49.49)	19000.00 (0.93)	63000.00 (3.09)	--	933000.00 (45.71)	16000.00 (0.78)	2041000.00 (100.00)
B. Swar	1086900.00 (38.90)	5000.00 (0.18)	151200.00 (5.41)	35700.00 (1.28)	1515000.00 (54.23)	- -	2793800.00 (100.00)
Rural Total (A+B)	**2096900.00 (43.37)**	**24000.00 (0.50)**	**214200.00 (4.43)**	**35700.00 (0.74)**	**2448000.00 (50.63)**	**16000.00 (0.33)**	**4834800.00 (010.00)**
II. Cities							
C. Rampur	102000.00 (5.28)	11000.00 (0.57)	- -	13000.00 (0.67)	1738000.00 (90.01)	67000.00 (3.47)	1931000.00 (100.00)
D. Swar	- -	- -	3500.00 (0.64)	12500.00 (2.29)	530800.00 (97.07)	- -	546800.00 (100.00)
Urban Total (C+D)	**102000.00 (4.12)**	**11000.00 (0.44)**	**3500.00 (0.14)**	**25500.00 (1.03)**	**2268800.00 (91.57)**	**67000.00 (2.70)**	**2477800.00 (100.00)**
District (Rural+Urban)	**2198900.00 (30.07)**	**35000.00 (0.48)**	**217700.00 (2.98)**	**61200.00 (0.84)**	**4716800.00 (64.50)**	**83000.00 (1.13)**	**7312600.00 (100.00)**

* Indicates income as agricultural labour, non-agricultural labour and from cattle and animal care, business, self-employed activity, service, artisanal activity, skilled intensive activity, household work, etc.

Note: Figures in parentheses denote per cent to total income.

Source: Based on the information collected from the field.

agriculture, from where 49.49 per cent of income has been generated. Next to this comes the income generated as the agricultural labour and non-agricultural labour, cattle and animal care, business, self-employed activity, service, artisional activities and household works. In Swar block, the agriculture has generated the income of 38.90 per cent, whereas income from business, services, artisanal work, etc. comes to 54.23 per cent. In rural total, the income from business, service, artisional work, etc. comes to 50.63 per cent, while that from the agriculture to 43.37 per cent (Table III.4).

In Rampur city, income generated from business, services, artisanal work, etc. comes to 90.01 per cent, while that from the agriculture to 5.28 per cent. In Swar city, the income from business, service, artisanal work, etc. comes to 97.07 per cent, while from poultry and birds to 2.29 per cent. In urban total, the income generated from business, service, artisional work, etc. comes to 91.57 per cent, while that from agriculture to 4.12 per cent. In the district (urban and rural total), 64.50 per cent of income have been generated from business, service, artisional work, etc., while to that from agriculture to 30.07 per cent (Table III.4).

As agriculture has been found second important source of income in rural and urban areas, it calls for the examination of households by land holdings. Analysis of Table III.5 shows that 77 households (or 40.10 per cent) in rural areas, while 7 (or 46.67 per cent) in urban areas have land between 1 to 2.5 acres. Further, 46 households (or 23.96 per cent) in rural and 4 (or 26.67 per cent) in urban areas have the land to less than 1 acre. Households having land between 2.5 to 5.0 acres are found to be 21.36 per cent in rural and to 13.33 per cent in urban areas. Further, households with land to more than 5.0 acres are found to be 14.58 per cent in rural, and to 13.33 per cent in urban areas.

In urban and rural total, a majority of households (84 or 40.58 per cent) have the land between 1 to 2.5 acres; 50 households (or 24.16 per cent) to less than 1 acre; and 43 households (or 20.77 per cent) between 2.5 to 5.0 acres of land. Notably, there are 30 households (or 14.49 per cent) are the large farmers, which have the land to more than 5.0 acres in rural (14.58 per cent) and in urban (13.38 per cent) areas of the Rampur district. This suggests that, irrespective of small size of land holding, a majority of households has generated the income from agriculture. This holds true in rural, urban and in the Rampur district as well. Higher land productivity appears to explain a higher income generating potential from agriculture in the Rampur district.

TABLE III.5

Distribution of Minority Households by Size of Land Holdings in Rural and Urban Areas: Rampur, 1997

Area	*Size of agricultural land owned*				
	Less than 1 acre	*1.0-2.5 acres*	*2.5-5.0 acres*	*Above 5.0 acres*	*Total*
Rural	46(23.96)	77(40.10)	41(21.36)	28(14.58)	192(100.00)
Urban	4(26.67)	7(46.67)	2(13.33)	2(13.33)	15(100.00)
Total	50(24.16)	84(40.58)	43(20.77)	30(14.49)	207(100.00)

Note: Figures in bracket denote per cent to row total.
Source: Based on the information collected from the field.

Table III.6 gives the average size of agricultural land owned by the households, average size of land leased out and leased-in in rural, urban and in the district. In rural areas, per household agricultural land comes to 2.97 acres, land leased out to 1.25 acres and that of land leased in to 2.41 acres. In urban areas, the per household agricultural land comes to 2.48 acres, while land leased out to 2.75 acres. However, the land leased in has been found to be non-existent in urban areas.

TABLE III.6

Absolute and Average Size of Land Owned, Land Leased-out and Leased-in in Rural and Urban Areas : Rampur, 1997

Area	Size of land holding					
	Agricultural land owned (acres)	*Average agricultural land owned (acres)*	*Land leased out (acres)*	*Average land leased out (acres)*	*Land leased in (acres)*	*Average land leased in (acres)*
Rural	570.25	2.97	7.50	1.25 *	33.80	2.41
Urban	37.25	2.48	11.00	2.75 **	--	--
Total	607.50	2.93	18.50	1.85	33.80	2.41

* Out of 192 households who have owned agricultural land, only 6 have leased out their land.

** Out of 15 households who have owned agricultural land, only 4 have leased out their land.

Source: Based on the information collected from the field.

In rural and urban total, the per household agricultural land owned comes to 2.93 acres, land leased out to 1.85 acres and that of land leased in to 2.41 acres. It appears that high productivity of land in rural as well as in urban areas by adopting the commercial crop (peppermint) has enhanced the income of minority households substantially.

We may empirically examine the levels of income in rural, urban and in district. Table III.7 distributes minority households in different income groups, such as, (i) upto Rs.8,000; (ii) Rs.8,001 to Rs.11,000; (iii) Rs.11,001 to Rs.18,000; and (iv) Rs.18,001 and above. In rural areas, a majority of households (156 or 47.85 per cent) is found under the income group of Rs.11,001 to Rs.18,000, while only 44 households (or 13.50 per cent) under the income group of upto Rs.8,000. In urban areas, a majority of households (79 or 45.41 per cent) is found within the income group of Rs.11,001 to Rs.18,000, while lowest number of households (28 or 16.09 per cent) within the income group of Rs.8,001 to Rs.11,000. In the district, of the total minority households (500), largest number of households (235 or 47.0 per cent) is found within the income group of Rs.11,001 to Rs.18,000, whereas, lowest number of households (76 or 15.20 per cent) upto the income group of Rs.8,000. Thus, a majority of minority household is found existing within the income group of Rs.11,001 to Rs.18,000 in the district.

TABLE III.7

Distribution of Households by Different Income Groups: Rampur, 1997

Area	*Number of minority households in different income groups*				
	Upto Rs.8000	*Rs.8001-R.11000*	*Rs.11001-Rs.18000*	*Rs.18001 and above*	*Total*
I. Blocks					
A. Bilaspur	16(13.11)	20(16.39)	43(35.25)	43(35.25)	122(100.00)
B. Swar	28(13.73)	44(21.57)	19(9.31)	19(9.31)	204(100.00)
Rural Total (A+B)	**44(13.50)**	**64(19.63)**	**156(47.85)**	**62(19.02)**	**326(100.00)**
II. Cities					
C. Rampur	30(22.73)	18(13.63)	50(37.88)	34(25.76)	132(100.00)
D. Swar	2(4.76)	10(23.81)	29(69.05)	1(2.38)	42(100.00)
Urban Total (C+D)	**32(18.39)**	**28(16.09)**	**79(45.41)**	**35(20.11)**	**174(100.00)**
District (Rural+Urban)	76(15.20)	92(18.40)	235(47.00)	97(19.40)	500(100.00)

Note: Figures in the bracket denote per cent to horizontal total.
Source: Based on the information collected from the field.

3. *Poverty Profile of Minority Households*

It may, however, be mentioned that defining poverty has always been treated as a complex problem. So far, it has not generally been accepted as to what criterion is the appropriate for distinguishing households below or above the poverty line. Researchers, have used either income or calorie intake criterion depending on the availability or suitability of information. In the present study, income per household as followed under Integrated Rural Development Programme (IRDP) has been used as a basis for distinguishing households below or above the poverty line. Under IRDP in 1994, households with income of Rs.11,000 or less have been considered below the poverty line. Owing to the readily availability of required information, we have followed the above approach of defining poverty level of rural and urban households. Thus, minority households have been distinguished below or above the poverty line in rural and urban areas in the Rampur district.

Table III.8 portrays the households below the poverty line across the villages and blocks in rural and urban areas. In Bilaspur block, out of 122 households, 36 households (or 29.50 per cent) are deemed below the poverty line. Poverty is found worse (66.66 per cent) in Kuiya village, while relatively less intense in Tal Mahavar village (17.39 per cent). In Swar block, out of 204 households, 72 households (or 35.39 per cent) are found below the poverty line. Across the villages, poverty is found worse in Millak Dundi (53.33 per cent), while less intense in Mirapur Meerganj (25.93 per cent).

Table III.8

Poverty Profile in Rural and Urban Areas: Rampur, 1997

Block and Villages	*Total households (No.)*	*Households below poverty line (No.)*	*Percentage of household below poverty line*
A. Bilaspur			
Ahro	28	8	28.57
Dhawni Hasanpur	19	4	21.05
Godhi	30	8	26.66
Kuiya	18	12	66.66
Tal Mahavar	23	4	17.39
Isa Nagar	4	- -	- -
Sub-Total	**122**	**36**	**29.50**

B. Swar			
Mandwa Hasanpur	29	12	41.40
Raipur	57	25	43.86
Mirapur Meerganj	27	7	25.93
Milak Dundi	15	8	53.33
Narpat Nagar	76	20	26.32
Sub-Total	**204**	**72**	**35.29**
Rural-Total (A+B)	326	108	33.12
C. Cities			
Rampur	132	48	36.36
Swar	42	12	28.57
Urban-Total	174	60	34.48
Grand-Total (A+B+C)	**500**	**168**	**33.60**

Source: Based on the information collected from the field.

In urban areas, poverty is found worse in Rampur city, where, out of 132 households, 48 households (or 36.36 per cent) are found below the poverty line. In Swar city, of the 42 households, 12 households (or 28.57 per cent) are deemed below the poverty line. Thus, it is apparent that poverty is more intense in Rampur than that in Swar city. In urban total, out of 174 households, 60 households or 34.48 per cent are found below the poverty line. Between rural and urban, poverty is found relatively less intense in the former than the latter one. In rural areas, households below the poverty line are found to be 33.13 per cent, while that in urban to 34.48 per cent.

In the district, out of 500 households, 168 households (or 33.60 per cent) are found living below the poverty line. A high intensity of poverty in urban than that in rural in Rampur district is mainly conditioned on account of lack of industrial base of the city economy. This city is mainly dominated by household works, self-employed activities, which do not seem to have a high income generating potential. Also the selection of blocks and villages in rural areas is not without bias. This is done by the District Minority Welfare Department, which does not seem to have followed any statistical procedure. It is felt during the field survey that villages selected in blocks are dominated by relatively prosperous minority households. Consequently, it has reflected the low poverty levels in rural areas. Needless to mention, it is a question of further empirical investigation for researchers by adopting more appropriate methods for examining the poverty in rural and in the urban areas.

Financial Linkage Pattern

1. Borrowing Pattern

Generally, linkages are examined in terms of input purchase, output disposal, purchase and sale of machinery within or outside of the district. Such types of inflow and outflow relationships are considered as technological linkages. However, given the framework of analysis, such types of linkages have not been examined in the present study on account of non-existence of required information. Instead, only financial linkages have been examined, which is described in Tables III.9, III.10 and III.11.

In rural areas during 1995-97, out of 326 households, 93 households (or 28.53 per cent) have taken loan. The amount of loan comes to 11.09 lakhs. It is found that a majority of households (43 or 46.24 per cent) has taken loan from commercial and non-commercial banks; 18 (or 19.35 per cent) from money lenders, 14 (or 15.05 per cent) from relatives and friends; 10 (or 10.75 per cent) from other Governmental Institutions/ Department; 5 (or 5.38 per cent) from traders; and to 3 (or 3.23 per cent) from other financial institutions. Thus, commercial and non-commercial banks followed by the money lenders, relatives and friends are the main sources of borrowing by the minority households (Table III.9).

TABLE III.9

Households Taken Loan From Different Sources in Rural and Urban Areas: Rampur, 1995-97

Sl.No.	*Particulars*	*Rural*	*Urban*	*Total*
1.	Total households (No.)	326(65.20)	174(34.80)	500(100.0)
2.	Household taken loan (No.)	93(76.23)	29(23.77)	122(100.0)
3.	Percentage of households taken loan to total households	28.53	16.67	24.40
4.	Amount of loan taken (Rs. in lakh)	11.09(73.78)	3.94(26.22)	15.03(100.00)
5.	Percentage of loan taken by households from different sources, of the total households loan taken:			
5.1	Commercial and non-commercial banks (No.)	43(46.24)	15(51.73)	58(47.54)
5.2	Other financial institutions (No.)	3(7.67)	1 (7.45)	4(7.60)
5.3	Minorities Finance and Development Corporation (No.)	--	--	--
5.4	Other Government Institutions/Departments (No.)	10(10.75)	1(3.45)	11(9.02)
5.5	Money lenders (No.)	18(19.35)	3(10.34)	21(17.21)
5.6	Traders (No.)	5(5.38)	4(13.79)	9(7.38)
5.7	Relatives and friends (No.)	14(15.05)	5(17.24)	19(15.57)
	Total households taken loan	93(100.00)	29(100.00)	122(100.00)

Source: Based on the information collected from the field.

In urban areas, out of 174 minority households, only 29 (or 16.67 per cent) have taken loan. Amount of loan comes to Rs.3.94 lakh. Of the urban households who have borrowed (29 households or 16.67 per cent), 15 households (or 51.73 per cent) have borrowed from commercial and non-commercial banks; 5 households (or 17.24 per cent) from relatives and friends; and to 4 households (or 13.79 per cent) have taken loan from traders. The money lenders have provided loans to only 3 households (or 10.34 per cent); and other Government institutions/departments and financial institutions to only 2 households (or 6.90 per cent). Thus, in urban areas, commercial and non-commercial banks, relatives and friends and traders have emerged as a major sources of lending (Table III.9).

In Rampur district, out of 500 minority households, 122 (or 24.40 per cent) have borrowed. The amount of loan comes to Rs.15.03 lakh during 1995-97. Of the minority households who have taken loan (122), 58 (or 47.54 per cent) have borrowed from commercial and non-commercial banks; 21 (or 17.21 per cent) from money lenders; 19 (or 15.57 per cent) from relatives and friends; 11 (or 9.02 per cent) from other governmental institutions/ departments; 9 households (or 7.38 per cent) from traders; and to 4 minority households (or 7.60 per cent) from other financial institution. It appears, therefore, that commercial and non-commercial banks, money lenders and relative and friends are the major sources of lending for the minority households. It is surprising, however, that Minorities Finance and Development Corporation has not extended loan to any minority households either in rural or in urban areas. May be that minority households are not aware about the financial assistance being extended by the Minorities Finance and Development Corporation (Table III.9).

2. Purpose of Loan

Table III.10 describes the purpose for which loan has been taken in rural and urban areas. In rural areas, a majority of households 40 (or 43.02 per cent) has borrowed for agricultural works/purchase of fertilizers and agricultural instruments. Next to this comes the initiation and expansion of business, for which 21 minority households (or 22.58 per cent) have taken loan. Thereafter comes medical treatment, house construction and marriage and other social ceremonies for which loan has been taken. It appears that a majority of households from minority community has borrowed for agricultural purposes followed by expansion of business and for meeting the medical requirement (Table III.10).

In urban areas, the purposes of loan are entirely different than that in rural areas. In urban areas, out of 29 households, who borrowed, 20 households (or 68.96 per cent) have taken loan for starting and expanding the business. Other purposes for which loan has been taken are found to be relatively less significant (Table III.10).

TABLE III.10

Households Taken Loan for Different Purposes in Rural and Urban Areas: Rampur, 1977

Sl.No.	*Particulars*	*Rural*	*Urban*	*Total*
1.	Total households (No.)	326(65.20)	174(34.80)	500(100.0)
2.	Household taken loan (No.)	93(76.23)	29(23.77)	122(100.0)
3.	Number and percentage of households taken loan to total households taken loan for:			
3.1	Medical treatment	15(16.13)	1(3.45)	16(13.10)
3.2	House construction	8(8.60)	3(10.34)	11(9.02)
3.3	Agricultural work/purchase of fertilizers/instruments	40(43.02)	1(3.45)	41(33.61)
3.4	Business and its expansion	21(22.58)	20(68.96)	41(33.61)
3.5	Marriage and other ceremonics	6(6.45)	2(6.90)	8(6.56)
3.6	Purchase of rickshaw and bullock-carts	3(3.22)	2(6.90)	5(4.10)
Total households taken loan		93(100.00)	29(100.00)	122(100.00)

Source: Based on the information collected from the field.

In Rampur district, out of 122 households taken loan, 41 minority households (or 33.61 per cent) have borrowed for agricultural work, purchase of fertilizers and agricultural instruments. An equal percentage of households have taken loan to initiate and expand their business activity. Also, 16 households (or 13.10 per cent) have taken loan for medical treatment, while 11 minority households (or 9.02 per cent) for construction of house. Thus, loan has been taken mainly for agricultural purposes, business and medical treatment (Table III.10).

Table III.11 records the various aspects of recovery of

loan in rural, urban and in district during 1995-97. In rural areas, out of 93 minority households loan taken, 76 (or 81.72 per cent) refunded the loan. Of the amount of loan taken, 42.20 per cent of loans were refunded. In urban areas, of the 29 households who borrowed, all of them refunded loans. Of the total loan taken, 59.39 per cent of loans were refunded. It seems that recovery of loan is higher significantly in urban than that in rural areas. In the district, out of 122 households, who have taken loan, 105 (or 86.07 per cent) refunded the loans. Of the total amount of loans taken, 46.71 per cent of them were refunded to the lending Governmental/non-governmental organizations, traders and relatives and friends (Table III.11).

TABLE III.11

Particulars about Recovery of Loan by Minority Households in Rural and Urban Areas : Rampur,1997

Sl.No.	*Particulars*	*Rural*	*Urban*	*Total*
1.	Total households (No.)	326(65.20)	174(34.80)	500(100.0)
2.	Household taken loan (No.)	93(76.23)	29(23.77)	122(100.0)
3.	Percentage of households loan taken to total households	28.53	16.67	24.40
4.	Amount of loan (Rs. in lakh)	11.09(73.78)	3.94(26.22)	15.03(100.00)
5.	Households who have refunded loans (No.)	76	29	105
6.	Percentage of households who refunded loan to loan taken households	81.72	100.0	86.07
7.	Amount of loan refunded (Rs. in lakh)	4.68	2.34	7.02
8.	Percentage of loan refunded to loan taken	42.20	59.39	46.71

Source: Based on the information collected from the field.

Summing Up

The foregoing analysis examines various economic characteristics of minorities in rural, urban and in the Rampur district. Of the total rural households, a majority of them is found engaged in farming. The minority households engaged as wage earners are found second, in order of importance. In urban areas, a majority of minority households is found engaged in business and trade, wage earning, household industry and in self-employed occupation. In Rampur city, a majority of household is found engaged as wage earners and cultivators, while in Swar city as self-employed and businessmen and traders. The importance of other economic occupations as employer of households from minorities are, however, found to be relatively less significant.

The minority population in rural areas has been found mainly engaged in household work. Next to this is agriculture, which has employed minority population considerably. In urban areas, household work has again appeared as an important economic occupation, which has employed a considerable proportion of minority population. In the district, household work, other economic occupations and agriculture have employed a majority of household members from minorities. It appears that household work, other economic occupations and agriculture are the important employment generating economic occupations.

Analysis has further been extended to examine the income level and poverty profile of minority households. Findings suggest that both income per household as well as income per capita are higher in rural than that in urban and in the district as a whole. Analysis, therefore, underlines that rural areas have a higher level of income per household as well as per capita than to those in urban areas in the Rampur district. Findings further reveal that poverty is less intense in the rural than that in urban areas. In the district, poverty is found less severe than the urban areas but marginally more intense than that in rural areas.

Analysis of linkages suggests that in rural areas, commercial and non-commercial banks, moneylenders, relatives and friends and other governmental institutions/

departments have extended loan to the rural minority households. In urban areas, commercial and non-commercial banks, money lenders and relatives and friends are the main sources of lending. In rural areas, loan has been primarily utilized for stimulating the agricultural work particularly for the purchase of the fertilizers and agricultural instruments and for the initiation and expansion of business.

In urban areas, loan has mainly been utilized for starting the business and for its expansion. In the district, loan has mainly been utilized for agricultural work, purchase of fertilizers and agricultural instrument and for starting the business and its expansion. Recovery of loan is found to be significantly higher in urban than that in the rural areas in the Rampur district. These are some of the economic aspects of the minorities dealt in this chapter. Chapter IV is devoted to examine the health and housing conditions of minorities in rural, urban and in the Rampur district.

4

Housing Characteristics and Health Conditions of Minorities

Introduction

Present chapter examines housing characteristics and health conditions of minorities. Housing characteristics are examined in terms of (1) housing conditions, and, (2) availability of room, kitchen and toilet facility, while health conditions in terms of (1) minority patients suffering from various diseases, (2) patients under treatment in different hospitals, (3) availability of medical facility and (4) child mortality among minority community. The empirical examination on above aspects has been considered important, because it will likely to explore the certain policy recommendations for improving the housing and health conditions of minorities.

Housing Conditions

1. Ownership and Structure of House of Minority Households

Table IV.1 portrays housing conditions of minority households in rural, urban and in the district. In rural, out of 326 minority households, 186 households (or 57.06 per cent) have owned ancestral houses, while to 131 (or 40.18 per cent) self-constructed houses. In urban areas, out of 174 households 63.22 per cent have the ancestral, while 26.44 per cent self-constructed houses. In the district, out of 500 minority households, 59.20 per cent have the ancestral, while to 35.40 per cent self-constructed houses. Thus, households with ancestral houses are found relatively more significant in urban than that in rural areas. However, minority households having self-constructed houses are found to be more significant in rural than that in urban areas. Also, households having rented houses are found to be more significant in urban (10.34 per cent) than to that in rural areas (2.76 per cent).

TABLE IV.1

Housing Characteristics of Minority Households in Rural and Urban Areas: Rampur, 1997

Particulars	*Rural*	*Urban*	*Total*
1. Ownership of house			
(a) Rented	9(2.76)	18(10.34)	27(5.40)
(b) Self-constructed	131(40.18)	46(26.44)	177(35.40)
(c) Ancestral	186(57.06)	110(63.22)	296(59.20)
Total	**326(100.00)**	**174(100.00)**	**500(100.00)**
2. Structure of house			
(a) Kutcha118(36.20)	30(17.24)	148(29.60)	
(b) Semi-kutcha	115(35.28)	71(40.81)	186(37.20)
(c) Pucca	93(28.52)	73(41.95)	166(33.20)
Total	**326(100.00)**	**174(100.00)**	**500(100.00)**
3. Number of rooms			
(a) One	23(7.06)	39(22.41)	62(12.40)
(b) Two	137(42.02)	88(50.57)	225(45.00)
(c) Three	123(37.73)	33(18.97)	156(31.20)
(d) Four and above	43(13.19)	14(8.05)	57(11.40)
Total	**326(100.00)**	**174(100.00)**	**500(100.00)**
4. Separate Kitchen			
(a) Yes	31(9.51)	62(35.63)	93(18.60)
(b) No.	295(90.49)	112(64.37)	407(81.40)
Total	**326(100.00)**	**174(100.00)**	**500(100.00)**
5. Latrine			
(a) Open (field)	115(35.28)	7(4.02)	122(24.40)

(b) Service	188(57.66)	124(71.27)	312(62.40)
(c) Flush system	23(7.06)	43(24.71)	66(13.20)
Total	**326(100.00)**	**174(100.00)**	**500(100.00)**
6. Garbage disposal			
(a) Near the house	176(53.99)	81(46.55)	257(51.40)
(b) Away from house	150(46.01)	93(53.45)	243(48.60)
Total	**326(100.00)**	**174(100.00)**	**500(100.00)**
7. Water drainage			
(a) Open/stagnant	137(42.03)	27(15.52)	164(32.80)
(b) Open and/or running	181(55.542)	131(75.29)	312(62.40)
(c) Closed	8(2.45)	16(9.19)	24(4.80)
Total	**326(100.00)**	**174(100.00)**	**500(100.00)**
8. Source of drinking water			
(a) Pond/Tank	--	--	--
(b) Well	--	--	--
(c) Handpump:			
(i) Government	142(43.56)	42(24.14)	184(36.80)
(ii) Private	180(55.21)	105(60.34)	285(57.00)
(d) Tap	4(1.23)	27(15.52)	31(6.20)
Total	**326(100.00)**	**174(100.00)**	**500(100.00)**
9. Source of lighting			
(a) Oil lamp/lantern	248(76.07)	36(20.69)	284(56.80)
(b) Electricity	78(23.93)	138(79.31)	216(43.20)
Total	**326(100.00)**	**174(100.00)**	**500(100.00)**
10. Fuel for cooking*			
(a) Waste	99(30.37)	2(1.15)	101(20.20)
(b) Coal	5(1.53)	35(20.11)	40(8.00)
(c) Firewood	320(98.16)	131(75.29)	451(90.20)
(d) Kerosene	130(39.88)	129(74.14)	259(51.80)
(e) Gas	7(2.15)	47(27.01)	54(10.80)
(f) Electricity	1(0.31)	5(2.87)	6(1.20)

* Indicates multiple responses by the minority households and therefore it does not add to 100.

Note: Figures within parentheses denote per cent to vertical total.

Source: Based on the information collected from the field.

As for the structure of house, of the total rural households (326), a majority of them (118 or 36.20 per cent) has the kutcha houses. Next to this comes the semi-kutcha houses, which are owned by 115 households (or 35.28 per cent). In urban, of the total minority households (174), a majority of households (73 or 41.95 per cent) has owned pucca houses. Next to this comes the semi-kutcha houses, which is owned by 71 (or 40.81 per cent) of minority households. In Rampur district, a majority of households (186 or 37.20 per cent) has owned semi-kutcha houses. Next, in order of importance, comes the pucca houses, which are owned by 166 households (or 33.20 per cent). Thus, kutcha houses in rural and pucca houses in urban have been the main sources of living for minority households. In the district, a majority of minority households was found living in semi-kutcha houses (37.20 per cent).

2. *Availability of Rooms, Separate Kitchcn and Latrine Facility*

As far the availability of rooms, a majority of minority households in rural and that in urban areas is found living in two room houses. In rural, 137 households (or 42.02 per cent), are found living in two room houses. The minority households with two room houses in urban are found to be 88 (or 50.57 per cent). In the district, of the total minority households (500), 225 households (or 45 per cent) are found living in two room houses. Households living in three room houses are found to be 123 (or 37.73 per cent). It implies that in rural, urban and in the district, a majority of households has generally been residing in two-room houses.

Study further examines the availability of separate kitchen facility in the houses of the households. It is reported that, in rural areas, out of 326 minority households, 295 households (or 90.49 per cent) do not have houses with separate kitchen facility. Such households are found to be

112 (or 64.37 per cent) in urban and to 81.40 per cent in the district. Thus, a majority of households has generally been residing in such houses, which generally do not have separate kitchen facility.

With regard to latrine facility, a majority of minority households (188 or 57.66 per cent) in rural areas has used service based toilet facility. Such households in urban areas are found to be 124 (or 71.27 per cent) and in the district to 312 (or 62.40 per cent. Open field has been used by 115 minority households (or 35.28 per cent) for this purpose in rural areas. Such households are found to be 7 (or 4.02 per cent) in urban; and to 122 households (or 24.40 per cent) in the district. In urban areas, out of 174 minority households, 43 (or 24.71 per cent) have been found using toilet based on flush system. Thus, in rural, urban and in the district, service based latrine has commonly been used by the majority of minority households. Next to this, comes the open field in rural and flush system in urban areas (Table IV.1).

3. Garbage Disposal, Water Drainage and Drinking Water

As for the garbage disposal, a majority of minority households in rural areas has disposed off garbage nearby their houses. The situation is all the more different in the case of urban households. Garbage is found disposed off away from their houses. In the district, a majority of minority household (257 or 51.40 per cent) has disposed off the garbage nearby their houses. Minority households disposing off garbage away from their houses are found to be 243 (or 48.60 per cent). It implies that disposing off the garbage near the house is a general practice in rural, whereas, while away from their houses in the urban areas. Also, disposing off the garbage nearby their houses is found to be a general practice in the district.

We have also examined the problem arising out of

water drainage in rural, urban and in the district. In rural, out of 326, a majority of minority households (181 or 55.52 per cent), has reported that water is open and running. Such households are 131 (or 75.29 per cent) in urban and to 312 (or 62.40 per cent) in the district. Water drainage problem is found applicable only to 137 households (or 42.03 per cent) in rural, 27 households (or 15.22 per cent) in urban and to 164 (or 32.80 per cent) in the district. However, 8 households (or 2.45 per cent) in rural; 16 (or 9.19 per cent) in the urban; and to 24 households (or 4.80 per cent) in the district have reported that flow of water is closed. Thus, water drainage appears to be a more severe in the urban than that in the rural areas.

As for the source of drinking water, out of 326 minority households in rural, 180 (or 55.21 per cent) have used water for drinking from privately owned hand pumps. Such households are found to be 105 (or 60.34 per cent) in urban areas and to 285 (or 57 per cent) in the district. Hand pumps owned by the government as a source of drinking water are found to be second, in order of preference. As much as 142 minority households (or 43.56 per cent) in rural; 42 households (or 24.14 per cent) in urban; and to 184 households (or 36.80 per cent) in the district have used water for drinking from the hand pumps owned by the government. It suggests that privately as well as government owned hand pumps are the main sources of water for drinking in rural, urban and in the Rampur district.

4. Sources of Lighting and Fuels for Cooking

As for the lighting, 76.07 per cent of minority households in rural areas are found using oil lamp/lantern for lighting. In urban areas, 79.31 per cent of minority households have reported that they have been using electricity for lighting. In the district, 56.80 per cent of minority households are found using oil lamp/lantern for lighting. In the district,

43.20 per cent of minority households are found using electricity for lighting. It appears that oil lamp/lantern is a major source of lighting in rural, while electricity in urban and oil lamp/lantern in the district.

We have also examined materials used for cooking by the minority households. A majority of minority households in rural (98.16 per cent), urban (75.29 per cent) and in the district 90.20 per cent has used firewood as a fuel for cooking. Next to firewood, kerosene and waste in rural; gas and coal in urban; and kerosene, waste, gas and coal in the district are found important fuels for cooking. Thus, firewood, kerosene and waste in rural; firewood, kerosene, gas and coal in the urban; and firewood, kerosene, waste, and gas in the district have been used as important fuels for cooking. However, firewood emerges as a single important fuel for cooking in rural, urban and in the district (Table IV.1).

Health Conditions

1. Level of Satisfaction by Minority Households

Table IV.2 portrays the views of minority households in relation to health conditions of their family members. In rural, out of 326, 238 (or 73 per cent) of households are found satisfied about the health conditions of their family members, whereas, 88 (or 27 per cent) are found dissatisfied. Block-wise also, a similar finding emerges. In Bilaspur, 54 per cent and that in Swar to 84 per cent of households are found satisfied, while remaining 46 per cent and 16 per cent in respective blocks are found dissatisfied.

In urban areas, 71 per cent of households are found satisfied, whereas, 29 per cent have expressed dissatisfaction. Within the cities, the level of satisfaction is found higher in Swar (81 per cent), than that in Rampur (68 per cent). Between the rural and urban, the level of satisfaction is found more significant in rural (73 per cent) than that in urban areas (71 per cent). Thus, health conditions of minority households are found more satisfactory in rural than that in urban areas. In the district, 72 per cent of minority households are found satisfied, while to 28 per cent have expressed dissatisfaction about the health conditions of their family members (Table IV.2).

TABLE IV.2

Responses of Minority Households about the Satisfaction of Health Conditions of their Family Members in Rural and Urban Areas : Rampur, 1997

Area	*Responses of minority households*		
	Yes (No.)	*No (No.)*	*Total (No.)*
A. Rural			
(a) Bilaspur	66(54.00)	56(46.00)	122(100.00)
(b) Swar	172(84.00)	32(16.00)	204(100.00)
Rural-Total	**138(73.00)**	**88(27.00)**	**326(100.00)**
B. Urban			
(a) Rampur	90(68.00)	42(32.00)	132(100.00)
(b) Swar	34(81.00)	8(19.00)	42(100.00)
Urban-Total	**124(71.00)**	**50(29.00)**	**174(100.00)**
Grand-Total (Rural+Urban)	**362(72.00)**	**138(28.00)**	**500(100.00)**

Note: Figures within parentheses denote per cent to horizontal total.

Source: Based on the information collected from the field.

2. *Minority Patients Suffering from Chronic Diseases*

Table IV.3 records information on patients suffering from chronic diseases and monthly expenditure incurred on medical treatment. A majority of minority patients is found suffering mainly from respiratory and stomach problems. In rural areas, out of 92 patients, 27 (or 29.35 per cent) are found suffering from respiratory and 24 (or 26.09 per cent) stomach problems. Other important diseases are bone and joints and tuberculosis as 15 (or 16.30 per cent) and to 10 (or 10.87 per cent) of patients are found suffering due to such diseases. Similarly, in urban areas, 22 (or 43.14 per cent), 11 (or 21.57 per cent) and to 5 (or 9.80 per cent) of minority patients are found suffering mainly from respiratory, stomach and tuberculosis diseases. In the district, 34.27 per cent of minority patients are found suffering from respiratory, 24.48 per cent from stomach, 12.58 per cent from bone and joints and to 10.49 per cent from tuberculosis.

Further, a majority of respiratory patients is found suffering to more than 3 years. This is found in case of minority rural patients (32.43 per cent) and that in urban patients (46.67 per cent). The respiratory patients suffering from to less than 3 years are found to be 27.27 per cent in rural and to 41.66 per cent in urban areas. Next comes the patients suffering from stomach problem. Such patients are found to be 16 (or 29.09 per cent) in rural and to 9 (or 25.00 per cent) in urban areas, which have been suffering to less than 3 years. Total minority patients suffering to less than 3 years are found to be 25 (or 27.47 per cent). Minority patients suffering to less than 3 years from stomach disease are found to be relatively more significant than to those suffering to more than 3 years in rural, urban and in the Rampur district.

Minority patients suffering from bone and joint problem from less than 3 years are found to be 8 (or 14.55 per cent) in rural, 3 (or 8.33 per cent) in urban and to 11 (or 12.09 per cent) in the district. Patients suffering from more than 3 years on account of this disease are found to be 7 (or 18.92 per cent) in rural and to 7 (or 13.46 per cent) in the district. In urban areas, however, patients suffering from bone and joints are found to be non-existent. Thus, bone and joint disease is found confined only in rural areas.

As for tuberculosis, patients suffering from more than 3 years are found to be 4 (or 26.66 per cent) in urban, equal

TABLE IV.3

Minority Patients Suffering from Chronic Diseases in Rural and Urban Areas Over Different Time Periods: Rampur, 1997

Chronic Diseases	*Minority patients suffering in:*			*Periods from:* *Less than 3 years*			*More than 3 years*			*Monthly expenditure per patient in:*		
	Rural (No.)	*Urban (No.)*	*Total (No.)*	*Rural (No.)*	*Urban (No.)*	*Total (No.)*	*Rural (No.)*	*Urban (No.)*	*Total (No.)*	*Rural (No.)*	*Urban (No.)*	*Total (No.)*
Respiratory problem	27 (29.35)	22 (43.14)	49 (34.27)	15 (27.27)	15 (41.66)	30 (32.97)	12 (32.43)	7 (46.67)	19 (36.54)	141.11	123.86	133.36
Bone & joint problem	15 (16.30)	3 (5.88)	18 (12.58)	8 (14.55)	3 (8.33)	11 (12.09)	7 (18.92)	- -	7 (13.46)	122.00	166.67	129.44
Stomach problem	24 (26.09)	11 (21.57)	35 (24.48)	16 (29.09)	9 (25.00)	25 (27.47)	8 (21.62)	2 (13.33)	10 (19.23)	201.25	191.81	200.28
Diabetic problem	5(5.44)	3(5.88)	8(5.59)	4(7.27)	2(5.56)	6(6.59)	1(2.70)	1(6.67)	2(3.85)	240.00	100.00	187.50
Tuberculosis	10 (10.87)	5 (9.80)	15 (10.49)	6 (10.91)	1 (2.78)	1 (7.59)	4 (10.81)	4 (26.66)	8 (15.39)	261.00	200.00	240.66
Paralysis	3(3.26)	- -	3(2.10)	2(3.64)	- -	2(2.20)	1(2.70)	- -	1(1.92)	250.00	- -	250.00
Eye problem	4(4.35)	3(5.88)	7(4.90)	1(1.82)	2(5.56)	3(3.30)	3(8.12)	1(6.67)	4(7.69)	125.00	100.00	114.28
Heart problem	4(4.35)	4(7.85)	8(5.59)	3(5.45)	4(11.11)	7(7.69)	1(2.70)	- -	1(1.92)	200.00	150.00	175.00
Total	92 (100.0)	51 (100.0)	143 (100.0)	55 (100.0)	36 (100.0)	91 (100.0)	37 (100.0)	15 (100.0)	52 (100.0)	177.50	149.12	167.38

Note: Figures under bracket denote per cent to vertical total.

Source: Based on the information collected from the field.

numbers (4 or 10.81 per cent) in rural and to 8 (or 15.39 per cent) in the district. Patients suffering from this disease from less than 3 years are found to be 2.78 per cent in urban, 10.91 per cent in rural, and to 7.69 per cent in the district. Thus, a majority of patients suffering due to this disease from more than 3 years is found to be relatively more significant in urban than that in the rural areas. However, patients suffering from this disease from less than 3 years are found to be more significant in rural than that in urban areas. Patients suffering from other diseases like, paralysis, eye problem and heart diseases in 1997 are found to be relatively less significant.

We have also examined the monthly expenditure per patient incurred on medical treatment. The per patient expenditure in rural areas has been found to be the lowest (Rs.122) on the treatment of bone and joint problem, whereas, highest (Rs.261) on treatment of tuberculosis. In urban areas, it is found lowest (Rs.100) on the treatment of diabetes and eye diseases, whereas, highest (Rs.200) on the treatment of tuberculosis. In the district, the monthly expenditure per patient is found to be lowest (Rs.114.28) on the treatment of eye diseases, whereas, highest (Rs.250) on the treatment of paralysis (Table IV.3).

3. Minority Patients Under the Treatment of Different Hospitals

We have also examined the nature of hospitals in which patients have been admitted for medical treatment in rural, urban and in the district. A close examination of Table IV.4 suggests that, out of 60 minority patients, 38 (or 63.33 per cent) in Bilaspur block 16 (or 50.00 per cent), out of 32, in Swar; and, 54 patients (or 58.69 percent), out of 92, in rural areas have been admitted in private allopathic hospitals for the medical treatment. As compared to this, the significance of other hospitals is found to be relatively less important. By and large, the same holds true in urban

TABLE IV.4

Minority Patients Admitted in Different Hospitals in Rural and Urban Areas: Rampur 1997

Patients under the treatment of	Rural			Urban			District		
	Bilaspur (No.)	Swar (No.)	Total (No.)	Rampur (No.)	Swar (No.)	Total (No.)	Rural (No.)	Urban (No.)	Total (No.)
District Hospital	4(6.67)	4(12.50)	8(8.70)	11(25.58)	1(12.50)	12(23.53)	8(8.70)	12(23.53)	20(13.99)
PHC/CHC	3(5.00)	4(12.50)	7(7.61)	- -	1(12.50)	1(1.96)	7(7.61)	1(1.96)	8(5.59)
Government Dispensary	- -	3(9.38)	3(3.26)	4(9.30)	1(12.50)	5(9.80)	3(3.26)	5(9.81)	8(5.59)
Private Allopathic Physician	38 (63.33)	16 (50.00)	54 (58.69)	21 (48.84)	2 (25.00)	23 (45.10)	54 (58.70)	23 (45.09)	77 (53.85)
Homeopathy	7(11.67)	1(3.12)	8(8.70)	4(9.30)	1(12.50)	5(9.80)	8(8.70)	5(9.80)	10(98.09)
Ayurvedic	3(5.00)	- -	3(3.26)	2(4.65)	1(12.50)	3(5.89)	3(3.26)	3(5.88)	6(4.20)
Unani	5(8.33)	4(12.50)	9(9.78)	1(2.33)	1(12.50)	2(3.92)	9(9.78)	2(3.93)	11(7.69)
Total	60(100.0)	32(100.0)	92(100.0)	43(100.0)	8(100.0)	51(100.0)	92(100.0)	51(100.0)	143(100.0)

Note: Figures under bracket denote per cent to vertical total.

Source: Based on the information collected from the field.

areas as well. For example, in Rampur, 21 patients (or 48.84 per cent), out of 43; in Swar 2 patients (or 25.00 per cent), out of 8; and in urban areas 23 patients (or 45.10 per cent), out of 51, are found admitted in private allopathic hospitals.

In the district, 77 (or 53.85 per cent) of patients, out of 143, are found admitted in the private allopathic hospitals. It appears that in rural, urban and in the district, a majority of patients has carried out their medical treatment in private allopathic hospitals. Other sources of medical treatment are, however, found to be relatively less significant in rural, urban and in the district (Table IV.4).

Relevant information on hospital facilities from secondary sources has also been collected for this purpose. The Chief Medical Officer, Rampur has provided the information, which has been collected by District Minority Welfare Department, Rampur. According to such information, it has been found that allopathic hospitals are the main centers of medical treatment. For example, of the 53 hospitals located in rural areas, a majority of

TABLE IV.5

Availability of Hospitals in Rural and Urban Areas: Rampur, 1997

Medical hospitals	*Rural (No.)*	*Urban (No.)*	*Total (No.)*
Allopathic hospitals	31(58.49)	9(45.00)	40(54.79)
Allopathic dispensaries	- -	4(20.00)	4(5.48)
Ayurvedic hospitals/dispensaries	9(16.98)	4(20.00)	13(17.81)
Unani hospitals/dispensaries	4(7.55)	2(10.00)	6(8.22)
Homeopathic hospitals/dispensaries	9(16.98)	1(5.00)	10(13.70)
Total	53(100.0)	20(100.0)	73(100.0)

Note: Figures within parentheses denote per cent to vertical total.

Source: Chief Medical Officer, Rampur, collected by Department of District Minority Welfare Department, Rampur, 1997.

them 31 (or 58.49 per cent) are allopathic. In the urban, of the 20 hospitals, 9 (or 45 per cent) are allopathic. In the district, out of 73 hospitals, 40 (or 54.79 per cent) are allopathic. The other types of hospitals in rural, urban and in the district are, however, found to be relatively less significant (Table IV.5).

Availability of Medical Facilities

We have also enquired from the minority respondents about the medical facilities available in (1) within the area, (2) at the block, (3) at the tehsil, and (4) at the district head quarters and about the nature of hospitals, such as, (1) district hospital, (2) government dispensary, (3) PHC/CHC, (4)private hospitals and (5) private physician. Such information across principal diseases in rural, urban and in the district has been recorded in Table IV.6. In rural areas, out of 326 households, a majority of them 208 (or 63.80 per cent) has reported that medical facilities for general ailment are available at the block level, while 33.13 per cent have felt that such medical facilities are also available within the area. General ailments are found generally treated under PHC/CHC centres.

With regard to MCH, a majority of minority households, i.e., 259 (or 79.45 per cent), has reported that such facility is available at the block level and is treated under PHC/CHC centres. For tuberculosis, the availability of medical facility is reported at the district head quarters, which is generally treated at district hospitals; for eye ailment, medical facility is reported to be available at the district headquarter, which is generally treated in the district hospitals.

For medical treatment of chronic diseases, a majority of minority households, 204 (or 62.58 per cent) have reported that medical facilities for such diseases are available at the district headquarter. Such diseases are treated under district hospitals. Private physicians for the treatment of

TABLE IV.6

Responses of Minority Households in Relation to Disease-wise and Area-wise Location of Medical Facilities and Availability of Different Kinds of Hospitals in Rural & Urban Areas: Rampur, 1997

Area and medical facilities in respect of:	*Responses of households in relation to location of medical facilities available*					*Responses of households in relation to kinds of hospitals*					
	Within area (No.)	*At block (No.)*	*At tehsil (No.)*	*At district headquarters (No.)*	*Total (No.)*	*District hospital (No.)*	*Govt. Dispensary (No.)*	*PHC/ CHC (No.)*	*Private physician (No.)*	*Private physician (No.)*	*Total (No.)*
A. Rural											
General ailments	108 (33.13)	208 (63.80)	10 (3.07)	- -	326 (100.0)	- -	35 (10.74)	177 (54.29)	4 (1.23)	110 (33.74)	326 (100.0)
MCH diseases	57 (17.48)	259 (79.45)	10 (3.07)	- -	326 (100.0)	- -	50 (15.34)	221 (59.33)	9 (2.76)	46 (14.11)	326 (100.0)
Tuberculosis	- -	- -	- -	326 (100.0)	326 (100.0)	275 (84.35)	4 (1.23)	- -	35 (10.74)	12 (3.68)	326 (100.0)
Eye ailment	- -	122 (37.42)	- -	204 (62.58)	326 (100.0)	162 (49.69)	6 (1.84)	5 (1.53)	88 (26.99)	65 (19.95)	326 (100.0)
Other chronic diseases	- -	122 (37.42)	- -	204 (62.58)	326 (100.0)	159 (48.77)	10 (3.07)	- -	56 (17.18)	101 (30.98)	326 (100.0)
B. Urban											
General ailments	174 (100.00)	- -	- -	- -	174 (100.00)	15 (8.62)	15 (8.62)	42 (24.14)	7 (4.02)	95 (54.60)	174 (100.00)
MCH diseases	174 (100.00)	- -	- -	- -	174 (100.00)	31 (17.82)	30 (17.24)	42 (24.14)	24 (13.79)	47 (27.01)	174 (100.00)

Area and medical facilities in respect of:	Responses of households in relation to location of medical facilities available					Responses of households in relation to kinds of hospitals					
	Within area (No.)	At block (No.)	At tehsil (No.)	At district headquarters (No.)	Total (No.)	District hospital (No.)	Govt. Dispensary (No.)	PHC/ CHC (No.)	Private physician (No.)	Private physician (No.)	Total (No.)
Tuberculosis	174 (100.00)	--	--	--	174 (100.00)	160 (91.96)	5 (2.87)	--	3 (1.72)	6 (3.45)	174 (100.00)
Eye ailment	174 (100.00)	--	--	--	174 (100.00)	110 (63.22)	9 (5.17)	--	13 (7.47)	42 (24.14)	174 (100.00)
Other chronic diseases	174 (100.00)	--	--	--	174 (100.00)	104 (59.77)	--	--	12 (6.90)	58 (33.33)	174 (100.0)
C. District											
General ailments	282 (56.40)	208 (41.60)	10 (2.00)	--	500 (100.0)	15 (3.00)	50 (10.00)	219 (43.80)	11 (2.20)	205 (41.00)	500 (100.0)
MCH diseases	231 (46.20)	259 (51.80)	10 (2.00)	--	500 (100.0)	31 (6.20)	80 (16.00)	263 (52.60)	33 (6.60)	93 (18.60)	500 (100.0)
Tuberculosis	174 (34.80)	--	--	326 (65.20)	500 (100.0)	435 (87.00)	9 (1.80)	--	38 (7.60)	18 (3.60)	500 (100.0)
Eye ailment	174 (34.80)	122 (24.40)	--	204 (40.80)	500 (100.0)	272 (54.40)	15 (3.00)	5 (1.00)	101 (20.20)	107 (21.40)	500 (100.0)
Other chronic diseases	174 (34.80)	122 (24.40)	--	204 (40.80)	500 (100.0)	263 (52.60)	10 (2.00)	--	68 (13.60)	159 (31.80)	500 (100.0)

Note: Figures under bracket denote per cent to vertical total.

Source: Based on the information collected from the field.

these chronic diseases are found to be second, in order of importance. Out of 326, 101 (or 30.98 per cent) of minority households feel that the treatment of these diseases has been undertaken by private physicians (Table IV.6).

In sharp contrast to above, the medical facility for all types of diseases in the urban areas has been found existing within the area itself. As for the kind of hospitals, a majority of minority households has reported that general ailments are treated by the private physicians, while tuberculosis, eye ailment and other chronic diseases at the district hospitals. In the Rampur district, 56.40 per cent of minority households are of the opinion that medical facility for general ailment is available within the area, which is treated under PHC/CHC and private physicians; and for MCH disease 51.80 pr cent of minority households feel that medical facility is available at the block level. Medical facility for tuberculosis, eye ailment and other chronic diseases is found generally available at the district headquarter and such diseases are treated generally under district hospitals (Table IV.6).

In urban areas, a majority of minority households feels that doctors should not be allowed for performing private practice. This particularly holds true in case of Rampur city. In Swar city, a majority of minority household feels that pathological tests in hospitals/PHC should also be started. In the district, a majority of minority household feels that doctors should be prevented from performing private practice. Also the adequate supply of medicines through the hospitals needs to be ensured. It emerges that "to open a dispensary at the village level" in rural, "the prevention of doctors from performing private practice" in the urban and in the district are the major steps required to be undertaken to improve the medical facilities (Table IV.8).

1. Level of Satisfaction for Medical Facilities by Minority Households

We have also investigated about the level of satisfaction with regard to medical facilities from the minority households. Such information has been recorded in Table IV.7. In rural areas, out of 326 minority households, 290 (or 88.96 per cent) are found dissatisfied in regard to medical facilities. The corresponding minority households are found to be 97.54 per cent in Bilaspur and to 83.82 per cent in Swar block. Similarly, in urban areas, out of 174 minority households, a majority of them 146 (or 83.91 per cent) are found dissatisfied in respect of medical facilities. Minority households dissatisfied in this respect are found to be 86.36 per cent in Rampur and to 76.19 per cent in the Swar city. Of the 500 minority households in the district (rural and urban), a majority of them 436 (or 87.20 per cent) are found dissatisfied in respect of medical facilities.

TABLE IV.7

Responses of Minority Households in Respect of Satisfaction of Medical Facilities in Rural & Urban Areas: Rampur, 1997

Area	*Households satisfied in respect of medical facilities*		
	Yes (No.)	*No (No.)*	*Total (No.)*
A. Rural			
(a) Bilaspur	3(2.46)	119(97.54)	122(100.00)
(b) Swar	33(16.18)	171(83.82)	204(100.00)
Rural-Total	**36(11.04)**	**290(88.96)**	**326(100.00)**
B. Urban			
(a) Rampur	18(13.64)	114(86.36)	132(100.00)
(b) Swar	10(23.81)	32(76.19)	42(100.00)
Urban-Total	**28(16.09)**	**146(83.91)**	**174(100.00)**
Grand-Total (Rural+Urban)	**64(12.80)**	**436(87.20)**	**500(100.00)**

Note: Figures within parentheses denote per cent to horizontal total.
Source: Based on the information collected from the field.

TABLE IV.8

Minority Households* Demanding Improvement in Respect of Medical Facilities in Rural and Urban Areas: Rampur, 1997

Steps required for improvement of medical facilities:	*Rural*			*Urban*			*District*
	HH in Bilaspur (No.) (N=119)	*HH in Swar (No.) (N=171)*	*HH in Total (Rural) (No.) (N=290)*	*HH in Rampur (No.) (N=114)*	*HH in Swar (No.) (N=32)*	*HH in Total (Urban) (No.) (N=146)*	*Total (Rural+ Urban) (No.) (N=436)*
To open a specialized hospital for treatment of chronic ailments at the block level	47 (39.50)	121 (70.76)	168 (57.93)	- -	5 (15.63)	5 (3.42)	173 (39.68)
To open a dispensary at the village level	87(73.11)	104(60.82)	191(65.86)	- -	- -	- -	191(43.81)
To appoint specialists in the existing hospitals	20 (16.81)	50 (29.24)	70 (24.14)	49 (42.98)	9 (28.13)	58 (39.73)	128 (29.36)
Proper medicines must be supplied through hospitals	69 (57.98)	55 (32.16)	124 (42.76)	80 (70.18)	20 (62.50)	100 (68.49)	224 (51.38)
Number of doctors must be increased in the hospitals	23 (19.33)	49 (28.65)	72 (24.83)	59 (51.75)	20 (62.50)	79 (54.11)	151 (34.63)
Facility for pathological tests in hospital/ PHC needs to be introduced	36 (30.25)	55 (32.16)	91 (31.38)	68 (59.65)	26 (81.25)	94 (64.38)	185 (42.43)
Doctors should be prevented from private practice	45 (37.82)	98 (57.31)	143 (49.31)	86 (75.44)	16 (50.00)	102 (72.34)	245 (56.19)
Others	30(25.21)	6(3.51)	36(12.41)	- -	- -	- -	36(8.26)

* Indicates multiple responses.

Note: Figures under bracket denote per cent to 'N' figure.

Source: Based on the information collected from the field.

Thus, medical facilities are found highly inadequate and dissatisfactory in rural, urban and in the district and therefore, it is important to look into the steps required for its improvement.

2. Steps Required for the Improvement of Medical Facilities

Table IV.8 records the steps required for improving the medical facilities. It is based on the multiple responses derived from the opinions expressed by the minority households. In rural areas, opening of a dispensary at the village level has been felt. Also, opening of the specialized hospitals at the block level for the treatment of chronic ailments has been felt essential by a majority of minority households. The above suggestion also holds true in case of Bilaspur and Swar block as well.

Child Mortality

Child mortality caused due to different diseases has been portrayed in Table IV.9. In rural areas, male child mortality upto one year of age is found due to cholera and tetanus. Out of total male mortality upto one year of age 14 or 35.71 per cent of death was occurred due to cholera and another equal percentage due to tetanus. Of the total male mortality from 1 to 5 years of age, 8 or 37.50 per cent were caused due to (1) cholera and (2) 25 per cent due to tetanus. Of the female mortality upto 1 year of age (13 or 30.77 per cent) were due to cholera; 23.08 per cent to tetanus; and to 23.08 per cent due to diarrhoea. Out of female mortality from 1 to 5 years of age (17), 29.41 per cent were due to diarrhoea and another 23.53 per cent due to whooping cough.

In rural area, out of male mortality from 1 to 5 years of age, 22 or 36.36 per cent were caused due to cholera and 31.82 per cent due to tetanus. Out of female mortality in all age group, 30 or 26.67 per cent were due to diarrhoea;

TABLE IV.9

Child Mortality During Last Five Years from Different Ailments in Rural and Urban Areas : Rampur, 1997

Ailments	Male/ female	*Child mortality in:* Rural			Urban			District		
		Upto 1 year (No.)	*1 to 5 years (No.)*	*Total (No.) (No.)*	*Upto 1 year (No.)*	*1 to 5 years (No.)*	*Total (No.) (No.)*	*Upto 1 year (No.)*	*1 to 5 years (No.)*	*Total (No.)*
Chorea	Male	5(35.71)	3(37.50)	8(36.36)	- -	1(50.00)	1(25.00)	5(31.25)	4(40.00)	9(34.62)
	Female	4(30.77)	3(17.65(	7(23.33)	- -	1(16.67)	1(14.29)	4(28.57)	4(17.39)	8(21.62)
Sub-Total	9(33.33)	6(24.00)	15(28.85)	- -	2(25.00)	2(18.18)	9(30.00)	8(24.24)	17(26.98)	
Pneumonia	Male	1(7.14)	- -	1(4.55)	- -	- -	- -	1(6.25)	- -	1(3.85)
	Female	1(7.69)	1(5.88)	2(6.67)	- -	- -	- -	1(7.14)	1(4.34)	2(5.41)
Sub-Total	2(7.41)	1(4.00)	3(5.77)	- -	- -	- -	2(6.67)	1(3.03)	3(4.76)	
Tetanus	Male	5(35.71)	2(25.00)	7(31.82)	- -	- -	- -	5(31.25)	2(20.00)	7(26.92)
	Female	3(23.08)	2(11.76)	5(16.67)	- -	2(33.33)	2(28.57)	3(21.44)	4(17.39)	7(18.92)
Sub-Total	8(29.63)	4(16.00)	12(23.08)	- -	2(25.00)	2(18.18)	8(26.66)	6(18.18)	14(22.22)	
Jaundice	Male	- -	1(12.50)	1(4.55)	1(50.00)	- -	1(25.00)	1(6.25)	1(10.00)	2(7.69)
	Female	1(7.69)	2(11.76)	3(10.00)	- -	- -	- -	1(7.14)	2(8.70)	3(8.11)
Sub-Total	1(3.70)	3(12.00)	4(7.69)	1(33.33)	- -	1(9.09)	2(6.67)	3(9.10)	5(7.94)	

Ailments	Male / female	Child mortality in: Rural			Urban			District		
		Upto 1 year (No.)	1 to 5 years (No.)	Total (No.) (No.)	Upto 1 year (No.)	1 to 5 years (No.)	Total (No.) (No.)	Upto 1 year (No.)	1 to 5 years (No.)	Total (No.)
Diarrhoea	Male	1(7.14)	1(12.50)	2(9.09)	1(50.00)	- -	1(25.00)	2(12.50)	1(10.00)	3(11.54)
	Female	3(23.08)	5(29.41)	8(26.67)	1(100.0)	1(16.67)	2(28.57)	4(28.57)	6(26.09)	10(27.03)
Sub-Total	4(14.82)	6(24.00)	10(19.23)	2(66.67)	1(12.50)	3(27.27)	6(20.00)	7(21.21)	13(20.63)	
Whooping Cough	Male	2(14.30)	1(12.50)	3(13.64)	- -	1(50.00)	1(25.00)	2(12.50)	2(20.00)	4(15.38)
	Female	1(7.69)	4(23.53)	5(16.67)	- -	2(33.33)	2(28.57)	1(7.14)	6(26.09)	7(18.92)
Sub-Total	3(11.11)	5(20.00)	8(15.38)	- -	3(37.50)	3(27.27)	3(10.00)	8(24.24)	11(17.46)	
Total	Male	14(100.0)	8(100.0)	22(100.0)	2(100.0)	2(100.0)	4(100.0)	16(100.0)	10(100.0)	26(100.0)
	Female	13(100.0)	17(100.0)	30(100.0)	1(100.0)	6(100.0)	4(100.0)	14(100.0)	23(100.0)	37(100.0)
Grand-Total		27(100.0)	25(100.0)	52(100.0)	3(100.0)	8(100.0)	11(100.0)	30(100.0)	33(100.0)	63(100.0)

Note: Figures under bracket indicate per cent to column male, female and grand total.

Source: Based on the information collected from the field.

23.33 per cent to cholera; and to 16.67 per cent to whooping cough. Thus, cholera, tetanus, diarrhoea and whooping cough have been found as a major disease due to which child mortality in minority community has occurred in rural areas.

In urban areas, out of male mortality upto one year of age, 50 per cent were due to jaundice and another equal percentage due to diarrhoea. Among the female mortality upto one year of age, all of them were due to diarrhoea. It seems that jaundice and diarrhoea have been the major cause for the male child mortality, while diarrhoea for the female child mortality. Of the male child mortality from 1 to 5 years of age, a majority of them was mainly due to cholera and whooping cough, while female death within the corresponding age group was due to tetanus and whooping cough. In urban areas in the all age group, whereas male mortality was mainly due to cholera, jaundice, diarrhoea and whooping cough (25 per cent due to each diseases), the female mortality was mainly due to tetanus, diarrhoea and whooping cough (28.57 per cent due to each diseases).

In the district of the male mortality upto 1 year of age (16), a majority of them died mainly due to cholera (31.25 per cent), tetanus (31.25 per cent), diarrhoea (12.50 per cent) and to whooping cough (12.50 per cent). Of the female mortality (14), a majority of them, i.e., 28.57 per cent died due to cholera; 21.44 per cent to tetanus; and to 28.57 per cent to diarrhoea. Similarly, of the male mortality from 1 to 5 years of age (10), 40 per cent of them were due to cholera; 20 per cent to tetanus; and another 20 per cent to whooping cough. Of the female mortality within the same age groups (23), 26.09 per cent of them were due to diarrhoea; equal percentage to whooping cough; 17.39 per cent to tetanus; and equal percentage due to cholera (Table IV.9).

In the district, of the male mortality in the all age

group 26 or 34.62 per cent were due to cholera; 26.92 per cent to tetanus; 15.38 per cent to whooping cough; and to 11.54 per cent to diarrhoea. Out of the female mortality in all age groups (37), a majority of them was due to diarrhoea (27.03 per cent); cholera (21.62 per cent); tetanus (18.92 per cent); and by equal percentage due to whooping cough. Out of the male and female mortality (63), 26.98 per cent of children died due to cholera; 22.22 per cent to tetanus; 20.63 per cent to diarrhoea; and to 17.46 per cent to whooping cough. The above analysis suggests that cholera, tetanus, diarrhoea and whooping cough were the main diseases due to which a majority of minority children upto 5 years of age died in Rampur district (Table IV.8).

Summing-Up

Present chapter examines housing characteristics and health conditions of minority community. In rural kutcha houses; in urban pucca houses; and in the district semi-kutcha houses are found owned by a majority of minority households. Also, in rural, urban and in the district, a majority of minority households has been found living in 2 room houses. In rural, urban and in the district, a majority of houses does not have separate kitchen facility. Service based latrine facility is found common in practice. Also, garbage is found disposed off nearby the house in rural, away from the house in urban and nearby the houses in the district. Water drainage problem is generally found more intense in rural than that in urban areas. Hand pumps owned by the individuals and by the government are found as a main source of drinking water in rural, urban and in the district. Oil lamps/lantern in rural, electricity in urban and oil lamps/lantern in the district are found as main sources of lighting. Firewood in rural, urban and in the district is found as a principal fuel for cooking.

As for the health conditions, a majority of minority

households in rural and in urban is found satisfied with respect of health conditions of their family members. However, the degree of satisfaction is found more in rural than that in urban areas. Those minority households who are dissatisfied have expressed the respiratory problem as cause for their dissatisfaction. This is true both in rural and in urban areas. Per patient expenditure incurred on medical treatment of all diseases comes to Rs.177.50 per month in rural, Rs.149.12 in urban and to Rs.167.38 in the district. Privately owned allopathic hospitals have been found as main centre for medical treatment of minority patients. This is carried out by private allopathic physicians in rural and urban areas.

As for the availability of medical facilities, medical facility for general ailment and MCH diseases in rural is found available at block level, while for tuberculosis, eye ailment and other chronic diseases at district head quarters. Whereas, general ailments and MCH diseases are treated at PHC/CHC centres, the treatment of other diseases is carried out at district hospitals. In urban areas, the medical facilities are available within the area itself. Whereas, general ailment and MCH diseases are treated considerably by private physicians in private hospitals, the treatment of other diseases is performed at the district hospitals. At the district level, medical facility for general ailment is available within the area, for MCH diseases at the block level and for tuberculosis, eye-ailment and for other chronic diseases at the district head quarters. The general ailment and MCH diseases are treated under PHC/CHC centres, while the treatment of other diseases is done under district hospitals.

In rural areas, those minority households dissatisfied due to inadequate medical facility demanded to open a dispensary at the village level and specialized hospital for treatment of chronic diseases at the block level. In urban areas, the respective minority households demanded the prevention of employed doctors from performing private practice. This is also held at the district level as well.

In rural areas it is revealed that the death of a majority of male child in all age groups has been caused due mainly to cholera and tetanus, while for females due to diarrhoea, cholera, tetanus and whooping cough. In urban areas, male child mortality in all age groups, has been caused due mainly to cholera, diarrhoea, jaundice and whooping cough, while for female due mainly to tetanus, diarrhoea and whooping cough. In the district, male child mortality in all age groups, has been caused due mainly to cholera and tetanus, while that for females to diarrhoea, cholera, tetanus and whooping cough. This chapter discussed the various aspects of housing characteristics and health conditions of minorities, the next chapter V is devoted to examine the impact of various rural development programmes on socioeconomic development of minorities.

5

Employment Structure, Welfare Programmes and Development of Minorities

Introduction

An attempt has been made in this chapter to examine: (1) the engagement of the minority households in different economic activities; (2) existing and proposed principal economic activities; (3) benefits accrued to the minority population from various development programmes and schemes; (4) the use pattern of community assets; and (5) overview of minority households to enhance their socio-economic development. The empirical examination of above aspects is felt important because this would likely to indicate the extent to which such developmental programmes have benefited the minority households in the Rampur district.

Minority Population Engaged in Different Economic Activities

Table V.1 describes the minority population engaged in artisonal, skilled and in self-employed activities. In rural areas, a majority of minority population 29 (or 53.70 per cent) is found engaged in self-employed activities. In urban areas, 152 (or 66.38 per cent) of minority population are found engaged as skilled workers. In the district, a majority of minority population 169 (or 59.72 per cent) is found engaged as skilled-workers. Thus, self-employed activity in rural and skilled-worker intensive activity in urban and in the district are found relatively more important economic activities (Table V.1).

TABLE V.1

Distribution Minority Population across Different Economic Activities in Rural and Urban Areas: Rampur, 1997

Activity	*Persons engaged in:*		
	Rural (No.)	*Urban (No.)*	*Total (No.)*
Artisans	8(14.82)	17(7.42)	25(8.83)
Skilled-workers	17(31.48)	152(66.38)	169(59.72)
Self-employed	29(53.70)	60(26.20)	89(31.45)
Total	54(100.0)	229(100.0)	283(100.0)

Note: Figures within parentheses denote percent to vertical total.

Source: Based on the information collected from the field.

1. Level of Satisfaction/Dissatisfaction of Minority Population Across Different Economic Activities

In Rampur district, 84 per cent of artisans, 60 per cent of skilled workers and to 39.33 per cent of self-employed are found dissatisfied. In all, 55.48 per cent of minority population have been found dissatisfied (Table V.2).

TABLE V.2

Minority Population by Satisfaction/Dissatisfaction Across Different Economic Activities: Rampur, 1997

Activity	*Persons whether:*		
	Satisfied (No.)	*Dissatisfied (No.)*	*Total (No.)*
Artisans	4(16.00)	21(84.00)	25(8.83)
Skilled-workers	68(40.24)	101(59.76)	169(59.72)
Self-employed	54(60.67)	35(39.33)	89(31.45)
Total	126(44.52)	157(55.48)	283(100.0)

Note: Figures within parentheses denote per cent to horizontal total.

Source: Based on the information collected from the field.

1.1 Reasons for Dissatisfaction

Table V.3 describes various reasons of dissatisfaction for artisans, skilled-workers and self-employed minority population. It provides multiple responses. A majority of minority artisans feels dissatisfied on account of low demand in the market, problem in marketing, irregular earnings, financial constraint and low margin of profit. Of the skilled-workers, a majority of them is found dissatisfied due mainly to exploitation by the middlemen, irregular earnings, lack of future prospects and the low wages. Of the self-employed, a majority of minority population is found dissatisfied on account of financial constraint and low margin of profit. It appears that low demand in the market and irregular earnings in the case of artisans; exploitation by the middlemen and irregular earnings in the case of skilled-workers; and financial constraint for the self-employed have been the main casual factors for dissatisfaction.

TABLE V.3

Reasons* for Dissatisfaction for Minority Population Across Different Economic Activities: Rampur, 1997

Reasons	*Artisans (No.) (N=21)*	*Skilled workers (No.) (N=101)*	*Self employed (No.) (N=35)*
Irregular earnings	13(61.90)	38(37.62)	7(20.00)
Exploitation by middlemen	--	74(73.27)	--
Low wages	--	29(28.71)	--
Lack of future prospects	7(33.33)	34(33.64)	6(17.14)
Low demand in the market/problems in marketing	18(85.71)	--	4(11.43)
Financial constraint in arranging working capital	12(57.14)	--	24(68.57)
Non-availability of raw material locally	6(28.57)	--	5(14.29)
High price of raw material	--	--	7(20.00)
Low margin of profit	11(52.38)	--	16(45.71)
Non-cooperative attitude of financial institutions/Banks	8(38.10)	--	10(28.57)
Others	--	--	--

* Indicates multiple responses.

Note: Figures within parentheses denote per cent to total 'N' figure.

Source: Based on the information collected from the field.

2. Possibility for Improving Economic Conditions of Minorities

We have also asked questions from the head of the minority households as to whether or not there exists any possibility for improvement in their economic conditions. This is described in Table V.4. A majority of the minority households is of the view that possibility for improvement in their economic conditions does not exist in rural, urban and in the district.

TABLE V.4

Possibility for Improvement of Economic Conditions of Minority Households From Present to Proposed Economic Activity: Rampur, 1997

Area	Possibility for Improving Economic Conditions			
	Yes (No.)	No (No.)	Not possible (No.)	Total (No.)
Rural	92(28.22)	178(54.60)	56(17.18)	326(100.0)
Urban	35(20.12)	104(59.77)	35(20.11)	174(100.0)
Total	127(25.40)	282(56.40)	91(18.20)	500(100.0)

Note: Figures within parentheses denote per cent to horizontal total.
Source: Based on the information collected from the field.

As for example, 54.60 per cent of minority households in rural, 59.77 per cent in urban and to 56.40 per cent in the district feel that possibility for improvement of their economic conditions does not exist, if they start new economic activities (Table V.4).

Present and Proposed Economic Activities and Financial Requirements in Proposed Activities

Table V.5 records present and proposed economic activities and average financial requirement to start the proposed economic activity. In rural areas, the principal employment generating activities are agriculture, non-agriculture and the cultivation, which respectively employed to 42.16 per cent, 34.31 per cent and to 17.65 per cent of minority population. In the rural areas, of the total minority population (102), a majority of them 41 (or 40.19 per cent) has proposed to start the general stores, which requires Rs.36,195. The 16 households (or 15.69 per cent) have preferred to start the cloth selling which may require Rs.46,937; 8 households (or 7.84 per cent) have preferred to start pan selling which may require Rs.12,875; 8 households (or 7.84 per cent) have preferred to start tea stall which may require Rs.11,000, etc. In rural areas, a person requires Rs. 32,755 to start a new economic activity.

In urban areas, of the minority population engaged in economic activities (39), 11 (or 28.21 per cent) are employed in bidi making; 7 (or 17.95 per cent) in karchob works; 4 (or 10.27 per cent) in rickshaw pulling; 3 (or 7.69 per cent) in non-agricultural activity; 2 (or 5.13 per cent) in TV/ Radio repairing, etc. Of the minority population employed in all activities (39), 8 (or 20.51 per cent) proposes to start general stores which may require Rs.27,250 per person; 6 (or 15.38 per cent) tea stall which may require Rs.11,666; 6 (or 15.38 per cent) motor binding which may require Rs.16,166; 4 (or 10.26 per cent) cycle repairing and parts shop which may require Rs.23,750; and 4 persons (or 10.26 per cent) electric shop which may require Rs.20,000 per person. In urban areas, a person requires Rs.22,026 to start a new economic activity.

In the district, out of 141 minority population, 43 of them (or 30.49 per cent) are found engaged as agricultural labour, 38 (or 26.95 per cent) as non-agricultural labour, 18 (or 12.76 per cent) in agriculture, 11 (or 7.80 per cent) in bidi making, 8 (or 5.67 per cent) in zari works, etc. Out of 141 minority population, 49 (or 34.75 per cent) have proposed to start a general store which may require Rs.34,734 per person; 18 (or 12.77 per cent) cloth selling which may require Rs.48,388; 14 (or 9.93 per cent) tea stall which may require Rs.11,285; and 13 (or 9.22 per cent) cycle repairing and parts shop which may require Rs.18,384 per person, etc. In the district, a person requires Rs.29,787 to start a new economic activity (Table V.5).

TABLE V.5

Present and Proposed Activities and Financial Requirement in Proposed Economic Activities in Rural and Urban Areas: Rampur, 1997

Present activities	*Persons engaged in:*		
	Rural (No.)	*Urban (No.)*	*Total (No.)*
Agriculture	18(17.65)	--	18(12.76)
Agricultural labor	43(42.16)	--	43(30.49)
Non-agricultural labour	35(34.31)	3(7.69)	38(26.95)
General stores	--	2(5.13)	2(1.42)
Cycle repairing	--	1(2.56)	1(0.71)
Tea stall	1(0.98)	--	1(0.71)
Zari work	1(0.98)	7(17.95)	8(5.67)
Bidi making	--	11(28.21)	11(7.80)
Kite making	--	2(5.13)	2(1.42)
Cap making	--	1(2.56)	1(0.71)
Carpentry	1(0.98)	1(2.56)	2(1.42)
Milk selling	2(1.96)	--	2(1.42)
Hair cutting	--	1(2.56)	1(0.71)
Rickshaw pulling	--	4(10.27)	4(2.84)
TV/Radio repairing	--	2(5.13)	2(1.42)
Compass making	--	2(5.13)	2(1.42)
Knife selling	--	1(2.56)	1(0.71)
Iron tools making	--	1(2.56)	1(0.71)
Wood making	1(0.98)	--	1(0.71)
Total	**102(100.0)**	**39(100.0)**	**141(100.0)**
General stores	41(40.19)	8(20.51)	49(34.75)
Cloth selling	16(15.69)	2(5.13)	18(12.77)
Pan selling	8(7.84)	1(2.56)	9(6.38)

Tea stall	8(7.84)	6(15.38)	14(9.93)
Hotel	6(5.88)	5(12.82)	11(7.80)
Atta chakki	9(8.82)	--	9(6.38)
Motor binding	--	6(15.38)	6(4.26)
Cycle repairing and parts shop	9(8.82)	4(10.26)	13(9.22)
Tailoring	- -	3(7.70)	3(2.13)
Electric shop	1(0.98)	4(10.26)	5(3.54)
Dairy	2(1.96)	- -	2(1.42)
Taxi/Tempo	1(0.98)	- -	1(0.71)
Diesel selling	1(0.98)	- -	1(0.71)
Total	**102(100.0)**	**39(100.0)**	**141(100.0)**
General stores	36,195.00	27,250.00	34,734.00
Cloth selling	46,937.00	60,000.00	48,388.00
Pan selling	12,875.00	23,000.00	14,000.00
Tea stall	11,000.00	11,666.00	11,285.00
Hotel	23,500.00	17,000.00	20.545.00
Atta chakki	41,111.00	- -	41,111.00
Motor binding	- -	16,166.00	16,166.00
Cycle repairing and parts shop	16,000.00	23,750.00	18,384.00
Tailoring	- -	23,666.00	23,666.00
Electric shop	15,000.00	20,000.00	19,000.00
Dairy	52,500.00	- -	52,500.00
Taxi/Tempo	50,000.00	- -	50,000.00
Diesel selling	90,000.00	- -	90,000.00
Total	**32,755.00**	**22,026.00**	**29,787.00**

Note: Figures within parentheses denote percent to vertical total.

Source : Based on the information collected from the field.

1. Advantages from Proposed Economic Activities

We also enquired about the advantages from the proposed economic activities in terms of employment/job work, marketing of products/services and earnings. Table

V.6 gives information on above aspects. In rural areas, general store, selling of cloth, selling of pan, atta chakki, cycle repairing and tea stall are found advantageous in terms of employment generation. In urban areas, such activities are tea stall and hotel. In the district, general store, selling of cloths, tea stall and hotel are found advantageous terms of employment generation.

As far the marketing of products/services, in rural areas, general store, selling of cloth, cycle repairing and parts shop have been found advantageous as 40 per cent, 15.79 per cent and to 9.48 per cent of minority population have expressed their opinions on this count. In urban areas, tea stall, motor binding, general store, hotel, cycle repairing and parts shop and electric shop have been reported to be advantageous in terms of marketing. In the district, general store, selling of cloth, cycle repairing and parts shop, tea stall, hotel and selling of pan have been felt advantagoous economic activities.

So far as earning is concerned, in rural areas, general store, selling of cloth, atta chakki, cycle repairing and parts shop, selling of pan and tea stall are found more advantageous economic activities in terms of earnings. In urban areas, general store, hotel, motor binding and tea stall have been found as more income generating activities. In the district, general store, selling of cloth, tea stall and cycle repairing and parts shops are found more advantageous in terms of income generation.

The above analysis suggests that from the view point of employment generation, general store in rural, tea stall in urban and general store in the district are the most advantageous economic activities. Similarly, from the view point of marketing, general store in rural, tea stall and motor binding in urban and general store in the district have been expressed as more important economic activities. With regard to earning view point, general store in rural,

TABLE V.6

Responses of Minority Household Members About the Advantages from Proposed Economic Activities in Rural and Urban Areas: Rampur, 1997

Proposed activities	Advantages in terms of								
	Employment / job work			*Marketing of products / services*			*Earnings*		
	Rural (No.)	*Urban (No.)*	*Total (No.)*	*Rural (No.)*	*Urban (No.)*	*Total (No.)*	*Rural (No.)*	*Urban (No.)*	*Total (No.)*
General stores	39(40.20)	3(17.65)	42(36.84)	38(40.00)	5(15.15)	43(33.59)	41(40.20)	8(20.51)	49(34.75)
Cloth selling	16(16.49)	- -	16(14.03)	15(15.79)	2(6.06)	17(13.28)	16(15.69)	2(5.13)	18(12.77)
Pan selling	8(8.25)	- -	8(7.02)	8(8.42)	1(3.03)	9(7.03)	8(7.84)	1(2.56)	9(6.38)
Tea stall	7(7.22)	6(35.29)	13(11.40)	7(7.37)	6(18.18)	13(10.16)	8(7.84)	6(15.38)	14(9.93)
Hotel	6(6.19)	5(29.41)	11(9.65)	6(6.32)	5(15.15)	11(8.59)	6(5.88)	5(12.82)	11(7.80)
Atta chakki	8(8.25)	- -	8(7.02)	8(8.42)	- -	8(6.25)	9(8.82)	- -	9(6.38)
Motor binding	- -	- -	- -	- -	6(18.18)	6(4.69)	- -	6(15.38)	6(4.26)
Cycle repairing and parts shop	9(9.28)	- -	9(7.89)	9(9.48)	4(12.12)	13(10.16)	9(8.82)	4(10.26)	13(9.22)
Tailoring	- -	3(17.65)	3(2.63)	- -	- -	- -	- -	3(7.70)	3(2.13)
Electric shop	1(1.03)	- -	1(0.88)	1(1.05)	4(12.12)	5(3.91)	1(0.98)	4(10.26)	5(3.54)
Dairy	1(1.03)	- -	1(0.88)	1(1.05)	- -	1(0.78)	2(1.96)	- -	2(1.42)
Taxi/Tempo	1(1.03)	- -	1(0.88)	1(1.05)	- -	1(0.78)	1(0.98)	- -	1(0.71)
Diesel selling	1(1.03)	- -	1(0.88)	1(1.05)	- -	1(0.78)	1(0.98)	- -	1(0.71)
Total	97(100.00)	17(100.00)	114(100.00)	95(100.00)	33(100.00)	128(100.00)	102(100.0)	39(100.0)	141(100.0)

Note: Figures under bracket denote per cent to vertical total.

Source: Based on the information collected from the field.

tea stall in urban and general store in the district have been reported to be more important economic activities.

2. Skill-Requirement

In order to make economic activities more profitable we have also asked relevant questions for improving the skills. Particularly, we have enquired about the improvement in training for artisans and self-employed. Training consists of (i) training in skills; (ii) training in entrepreneurship/ management; (iii) training in marketing; (iv) training in accounting; and (v) training in reducing the cost of production. Table V.7 records multiple responses on these aspects.

In rural areas, cent per cent artisans require training in skills; 66.67 per cent in reducing the cost of production; and to 33.33 per cent in entrepreneurship/management. However, artisans in rural areas have not felt the need for training in marketing and accounting. Self-employed personnel in rural areas, have needed training in skills; reducing the cost of production; accounting; and in entrepreneurship/management. Of the total self-employed persons (21), 42.86 per cent required training in skill improvement; 38.09 per cent in reducing the cost of production, 33.33 per cent in accounting; and to 23.81 per cent in entrepreneurship/management.

In urban areas, a majority of artisans (80 per cent) required training in skill development, while to 53.33 per cent in reducing the cost of production. Among the self-employed personnel, 69.56 per cent felt the need for training in entrepreneurship/ management; 26.09 per cent in marketing; 21.74 per cent in accounting; and to 10.87 per cent in skill development.

In rural and urban total, out of 21, a majority of artisans, i.e. 85.71 per cent required training in skill development, while to 57.14 per cent in reducing the cost

TABLE V.7

Training Required by Artisans* and Self-Employed* in Rural, Urban and in the District: Rampur, 1997

Training	Need for improving the skills in:					
	Rural		*Urban*		*Total*	
	Artisans (No.)	*Self-employed (No.)*	*Artisans (No.)*	*Self-employed (No.)*	*Artisans (No.)*	*Self-employed (No.)*
Training in skills	6(100.0)	9(42.86)	12(80.00)	5(10.87)	18(85.71)	14(20.89)
Training in entrepreneurship/ management	2(33.33)	5(23.81)	- -	32(69.56)	2(9.52)	37(55.22)
Training in marketing	- -	- -	- -	12(26.09)	- -	12(17.81)
Training in accounting	- -	7(33.33)	- -	10(21.74)	- -	17(25.37)
Training in reducing the cost of production	4(66.67)	8(38.09)	8(53.33)	- -	12(57.14)	8(11.94)
N=	6(100.0)	21(100.0)	15(100.0)	46(100.0)	21(100.0)	67(100.0)

* Indicates multiple responses.

N = Indicates number of artisans and self-employed personnel separately.

Note: Figures under bracket denote per cent to figure 'N'.

Source: Based on the information collected from the field.

of production. Within the self-employed personnel, out of 67, a majority of them (55.22 per cent) has required training in entrepreneurship/management followed by training in accounting (25.37 per cent) and in skill development (20.89 per cent). It emerges that artisans in rural and urban areas, required training in improvement of their skills. Self-employed personnel in rural required training in skill development and that in urban in entrepreneurship/management. In the district, artisans felt the need of training in skill development, whereas, self-employed in improvement of entrepreneurship/ management.

3. Financial and Training Required by Un-employed Youth

We have also enquired about the financial and training requirements for the un-employed youth. Multiple responses are recorded in Table V.8 on above aspects. In rural areas, out of 46 un-employed youths, 78.26 per cent felt the need for finance, while to 34.78 per cent for training. In urban areas, out of 26 un-employed youths, 82.31 per cent required finance, while to 26.92 per cent felt the need for training. In rural and urban total, out of 72 un-

TABLE V.8

Responses of Unemployed Youth on Supports* Required for Improving Their Economic Conditions in Rural and Urban Areas: Rampur, 1997

Area	*Unemployed youth ("N")*	*Financial support (No.)*	*Training required (No.)*
Rural	46(100.00)	36(78.26)	16(34.78)
Urban	26(100.00)	24(82.31)	7(26.92)
Total	72(100.00)	60(83.33)	23(31.94)

* Indicates multiple responses.

Note: Figures within parentheses denote per cent to un-employed youth "N" figure.

Source: Based on the information collected from the field.

employed youths, 83.33 per cent required finance, while to 31.94 per cent training. It appears that for improving the economic conditions need for finance is more important and urgent than that for training for the un-employed youths.

3.1 Skill Required by Under-employed Youths Across Principal Economic Activities

Table V.9 gives educational skill required by under-employed youths across different economic activities. In rural areas, a majority of under-employed youths has required educational skill in zari work followed by tailoring and in repairing. In urban areas, a majority of under-employed youth has required educational skill in zari work, repairing, blacksmithy and in tailoring. In the district, a majority of under-employed youths required educational skill in zari work, repairing, tailoring and blacksmithy. It appears that educational skill is an important requirement for zari works, tailoring, repairing and in blacksmithy.

TABLE V.9

Responses* of Under-employed Youths about the Requirement of Educational Skills in Different Economic Activities in Rural and Urban Areas: Rampur, 1997

Technical / educational skills required in:	*Rural (No.)*	*Urban (No.)*	*Total (No.)*
Tailoring	2(16.67)	3(4.76)	5(6.67)
Electrical/mechanical work	- -	2(3.17)	2(2.67)
Zari work	4(33.33)	7(11.11)	11(14.67)
Repairing	1(8.33)	5(7.94)	6(8.00)
Blacksmithy	- -	4(6.35)	4(5.33)
Cap making	- -	1(1.59)	1(1.33)
N=	12(100.0)	63(100.0)	75(100.0)

* Indicates multiple responses.

Note: Figures within parentheses denote per cent to "N" figure.

Source: Based on the information collected from the field.

TABLE V.10

Responses* by Self-employed and Under-employed Youths about the Supports in Rural and Urban Areas: Rampur, 1997

Supports	*Rural*		*Urban*		*Total*	
	Under-employed (No.)	*Self-employed (No.)*	*Under-employed (No.)*	*Self-employed (No.)*	*Under-employed (No.)*	*Self-employed (No.)*
Fertilizer and seeds	37(66.07)	--	--	--	37(61.66)	--
Awareness about self-employment generating programme/schemes	12(21.43)	4(33.33)	3(75.00)	24(38.09)	15(25.00)	28(37.33)
Financial support for opening business	41(73.21)	8(66.67)	4(100.0)	27(42.86)	45(100.00)	35(46.66)
Training	18(32.14)	6(50.00)	2(50.00)	18(28.57)	20(33.33)	24(32.00)
N=	56(100.0)	12(100.0)	4(100.0)	63(100.0)	60(100.0)	75(100.0)

* Indicates multiple responses.

Note: Figures within parentheses denote per cent to "N" figure.

Source: Based on the information collected from the field.

Table V.10 portrays supports required by under-employed and self-employed personnel. In rural areas, underemployed youths have felt the need for finance, fertilizer and seeds. The awareness about self-employment and training are, however, found to be relatively less important. As far self-employed personnel, 66.67 per cent required finance, while to 50 per cent training.

In urban areas, financial support followed by awareness about self-employment generating schemes and training are found important. However, the need for fertilizer and seeds has been found to be non-existent for the self-employed urban youths. In the district, under-employed youths have felt the need for finance, seeds and fertilizers. Next to above comes the need for training and awareness about the employment generating programmes. Self-employed youths required financial support followed by awareness about the employment generating programme and the training.

Impact of Development Programmes

We have also recorded the responses of minority households about the benefits accrued from various development programmes/schemes. Table V.11 summarises the views expressed by minority households. In rural areas, a majority of households (62.27 per cent) feels that development programmes/schemes have not benefitted to the minorities. However, 37.73 per cent of the minority households feel that development programmes/schemes have benefitted to them.

In urban areas, a majority of households (67.24 per cent) is of the opinion that development programmes and schemes have not been beneficial and, therefore, they have not made a positive contribution in the economic upliftment of minorities. However, 32.76 per cent of minority households are of the view that development programmes/schemes have benefitted to the minority community. In the district, 64 per cent of minority households feel that development programmes/schemes are not beneficial to them, whereas, 36 per cent feel otherwise. Thus, development programmes/schemes as an instrument of economic upliftment for minorities have not been found satisfactory. A detailed look into the success/failure of development programmes/ schemes across males and females would likely to provide a more clear view.

TABLE V.11

Responses of Minority Households about the Benefit from Development Programmes/Schemes in Rural and Urban Areas: Rampur, 1997

Area	*Whether minority households benefitted from programmes / schemes*		
	Yes (No.)	*No (No.)*	*Total (No.)*
A. Blocks			
(a) Bilaspur	51(41.80)	71(58.20)	122(100.00)
(b) Swar	72(35.29)	132(64.71)	204(100.00)
Rural-Total	**123(37.73)**	**203(62.27)**	**326(100.00)**
B. Cities			
(a) Rampur	46(34.85)	86(65.15)	132(100.00)
(b) Swar	11(26.19)	31(73.81)	42(100.00)
Urban-Total	**57(32.76)**	**117(67.24)**	**174(100.00)**
Grand-Total (Rural+Urban)	**180(36.00)**	**320(64.00)**	**500(100.00)**

Note: Figures within parentheses denote per cent to horizontal total.
Source: Based on the information collected from the field.

Table V.12 records male and female minority beneficiaries across various development programmes. In rural areas, 63.56 per cent of males and to 36.44 per cent of females have been found benefitted from Total Literacy Campaign. Male beneficiaries from Computer Education Programme under Skill Development Programme are found to be 66.67 per cent, while that of female beneficiaries to

33.33 per cent. The main beneficiaries from Non-Formal Education Programme are the males. However, female beneficiaries from this programme have been found to be non-existent. In all, 64.23 per cent of males and to 35.77 per cent of females have been found to be benefitted from all development programmes. In urban areas, male and female beneficiaries from Total Literacy Campaign are found to be equal proportionately (i.e. 50 per cent each). However, only males are found benefitted from coaching for competitive examination. In urban total, 55 per cent of males and to 45 per cent of females are found benefitted from all development programmes.

In the district, 61.76 per cent of males and to 38.24 per cent of females are found benefitted from Total Literacy Campaign, while from Non-Formal Education and Coaching for Competitive Examinations only males are found benefitted. Also, 66.67 per cent of males and to 33.33 per cent of females are found benefitted from Computer Education, which is a part of skill development programme. In the district 62.94 per cent of males and to 37.06 per cent of females are found benefitted from all development programmes. It is interesting that in rural areas 23.62 per cent of minority households have been benefitted, while in urban areas it comes to 7.47 per cent. Thus, development programmes have provided more benefits in rural than to that in urban areas (Table V.12).

Information on persons benefitted from different development programmes has also been collected from office of Chief Development Officer by the Department of District Minority Welfare, Rampur. It is recorded in Table V.13. We find that in 1997, applicants under IRDP are 956, DWCRA 750, TRYSEM 440, NRY 397, PMRY 471 and under Nirbal Varg Avas Yojana to 364 in the Rampur district. Beneficiaries under IRDP, are found to be 585 (or 61.19 per cent); TRYSEM 230 (or 52.27 per cent); PMRY 29 (or 6.16 per cent); and under Nirbal Varg Avas Yojana

TABLE V.12

Minority Male and Female Beneficiaries by Various Development Programmes in Rural and Urban Areas: Rampur, 1997

Programmes/ schemes	*Number of persons benefitted in:*								
	Rural			*Urban*			*Total*		
	Male (No.)	*Female (No.)*	*Total (No.)*	*Male (No.)*	*Female (No.)*	*Total (No.)*	*Male (No.)*	*Female (No.)*	*Total (No.)*
Total Literacy Campaign	75(63.56)	43(36.44)	118(100.0)	9(50.00)	9(50.00)	18(100.0)	84(61.76)	52(38.24)	136(100.0)
Non-Formal Education	2(100.0)	- -	2(100.0)	- -	- -	- -	2(100.0)	- -	2(100.0)
Coaching for Competitive Examinations	- -	- -	- -	2(100.0)	- -	2(100.0)	2(100.0)	- -	2(100.0)
Skill Development Programmes of Minority Finance and Development Corporation:									
(a) Computer Education	2(66.67)	1(33.33)	3(100.00)	- -	- -	- -	2(66.67)	1(33.33)	3(100.00)
(b) Stenography	- -	- -	- -	- -	- -	- -	- -	- -	- -
All	79(64.23)	44(35.77)	123(100.00)	11(55.00)	9(45.00)	20(100.0)	90(62.94)	53(37.06)	143(100.0)

Note: Figures under bracket denote per cent of total in rural, urban and in the district.

Source: Based on the information collected from the field.

to 316 (or 86.81 per cent). Under IRDP, of the minority applicants, 63.78 per cent are the beneficiaries. Under TRYSEM, of the total applicants, 56.79 per cent are the beneficiaries; under PMRY 7.61 per cent are the beneficiaries; and under Nirbal Varg Avas Yojana all minority applicants have been found to be the beneficiaries. Thus, minorities have received benefits from IRDP, TRYSEM, Nirbal Varg Avas Yojana and PMRY. Remaining programmes are yet to play their roles for the development of minority community.

TABLE V.13

Applicants and Beneficiaries from Various Development Programmes: Rampur, 1997

Programmes / schemes	*Total*		*Minorities*	
	Applicants (No.)	*Beneficia ries* (No.)*	*Applicants (No.)*	*Beneficia- ries** (No.)*
IRDP	956	585(61.19)	312	199(63.78)
DWCRA	750	- -	270	- -
TRYSEM	440	230(52.27)	160	92(56.79)
NRY	397	- -	- -	- -
PMRY	471	29(6.16)	92	7(7.61)
Nirbal Varg Avas Yojana	364	316(86.81)	28	28(100.0)

Note: * Figures under bracket denote per cent to total applicants.
** Figures under bracket denote per cent to total minority applicants.

Source: Based on the information collected from the District Minority Welfare Office and from the Chief Development Officer, Rampur, 1997.

Table V.14 gives information on programmes and schemes by agencies/ organizations and types of benefits received by the members of the minority households. In rural areas, a majority of household members has received benefits in terms of employment by Gram Sabha through employment generating programmes. Loans and subsidies have been received by the members of the minority households through banks under self-employment in

TABLE V.14

Responses of Minority Population Across Different Economic Development Programmes, Agencies/Organizations and Benefits in Rural and Urban Areas: Rampur, 1997

Area / Programmes / Schemes	*Agency / Organization*									
	Block / DRDA (No.)	*Bank (No.)*	*Gram sabha (No.)*	*Industries department (No.)*	*Export corporation (No.)*	*Handloom corporation (No.)*	*Handicraft Board / Directorate (No.)*	*Khadi Gramodyod Board (No.)*	*Minority's Finance & Development Corpn. (No.)*	*Total (No.)*
Rural										
Employment generating programme	--	--	110	-- (100.0)	--	--	--	--	--	110 (100.0)
Self-employment in skilled activity	--	--	--	--	--	--	--	--	--	--
Self-employment in artisanal/ handicraft/ household activity	1 (33.33)	2 (66.67)	--	--	--	--	--	--	--	3 (100.0)
Self-employment in trade/business	9 (100.0)	--	--	--	--	--	--	--	--	9 (100.0)
Self-employment in service activity	--	--	--	--	--	--	--	--	--	--
Manufacturing activity	--	--	--	--	--	--	--	--	--	--
Export	--	--	--	--	--	--	--	--	--	--
Seasonal activity	--	1 (100.0)	--	--	--	--	--	--	--	1 (100.0)
Sub-Total	10 (8.13)	3 (2.44)	110 (89.43)	--	--	--	--	--	--	123 (100.0)

Area / Programmes / Schemes	Agency / Organization: Block / DRDA (No.)	Bank (No.)	Gram sabha (No.)	Industries depart ment (No.)	Export corpora-tion (No.)	Handloom corpora tion (No.)	Handi-craft Board / Directo-rate (No.)	Khadi Gramod-yod Board (No.)	Minority's Finance & Development Corpn. (No.)	Total (No.)
Urban										
Employment generating programme	7 (100.0)	--		--	--	--	--	--	--	7 (100.0)
Self-employment in skilled activity	--	32 (100.0)	--	--	--	--	--	--	-- (100.0)	32
Self-employment in artisanal/ handicraft/ household activity	--	9 (100.0)	--	--	--	--	--	--	--	9 (100.0)
Self-employment in trade/business	--	9 (100.0)	--	--	--	--	--	--	--	9 (100.0)
Self-employment in service activity	--	--	--	--	--	--	--	--	--	--
Manufacturing activity	--	--	--	--	--	--	--	--	--	--
Export	--	--	--	--	--	--	--	--	--	--
Seasonal activity	--	--	--	--	--	--	--	--	--	--
Sub-Total	7 (14.00)	50 (86.00)	--	--	--	--	--	--	--	57 (100.0)
District										
Employment generating programme	7 (5.98)	--	110 (94.02)	--	--	--	--	--	--	117 (100.0)
Self-employment in skilled activity	--	32 (100.00)	--	--	--	--	--	--	--	32 (100.00)

Self-employment in artisanal/ handicraft/ household activity	1 (8.33)	11 (91.67)	--	--	--	--	--	--	--	12 (100.0)
Self-employment in trade/business	9 (50.0)	9 (50.0)	--	--	--	--	--	--	--	18 (100.0)
Self-employment in service activity	--	--	--	--	--	--	--	--	--	--
Manufacturing activity	--	--	--	--	--	--	--	--	--	--
Export	--	--	--	--	--	--	--	--	--	--
Seasonal activity	--	1 (100.0)	--	--	--	--	--	--	--	1 (100.0)
Total	17 (9.44)	53 (29.44)	110 (61.12)	--	--	--	--	--	--	180 (100.0)

Areas / Programmes / Schemes	Types of benefits received							
	Employ-ment (No.)	Loan (No.)	Loan and Subsidy (No.)	Training under TRYSEM (No.)	Training in skill devel-opment (No.)	Supply of raw materials at con-trol rate (No.)	Assistance in marketing of prroducts (No.)	Total No
Rural								
Employment generating programme	110 (100.0)	- -	- -	- -	- -	- -	- -	110 (100.0)
Self-employment in skilled activity	- -	- -	- -	- -	- -	- -	- -	- -
Self-employment in artisanal/ handicraft/ household activity	- -	- -	3 (100.0)	- -	- -	- -	- -	3 (100.0)
Self-employment in trade/business	- -	- -	9 (100.0)	- -	- -	- -	- -	9 (100.0)
Self-employment in service activity	- -	- -	- -	- -	- -	- -	- -	- -
Manufacturing activity	- -	- -	- -	- -	- -	- -	- -	- -
Export	- -	- -	- -	- -	-	- -	- -	- -
Seasonal activity	- -	- -	1 (100.0)	- -	- -	- -	- -	1 (100.0)
Sub-Total	110 (89.43)	- -	13 (10.57)					123 (100.0)
Urban								
Employment generating programme	3 (42.86)	- -	4 (57.74)	- -	- -	- -	- -	7 (100.0)
Self-employment in skilled activity	- -	- -	26 (81.25)	- -	6 (18.75)	- -	- -	32 (100.0)
Self-employment in artisanal/ handicraft/ household activity	- -	- -	9 (100.0)	- -	- -	- -	- -	9 (100.0)
Self-employment in trade/ business	2 (22.22)	3 (33.33)	4 (44.45)	- -	- -	- -	- -	9 (100.0)

Areas / Programmes / Schemes	Types of benefits received: Employment (No.)	Loan (No.)	Loan and Subsidy (No.)	Training under TRYSEM (No.)	Training in skill development (No.)	Supply of raw materials at control rate (No.)	Assistance in marketing of prroducts (No.)	Total No
Self-employment in service activity	--	--	--	--	--	--	--	--
Manufacturing activity	--	--	--	--	--	--	--	--
Export	--	--	--	--	--	--	--	--
Seasonal activity	--	--	--	--	--	--	--	--
Sub-Total	5 (8.77)	3 (5.26)	43 (75.44)	--	6 (10.53)	--	--	57 (100.0)
District								
Employment generating programme	113 (96.58)	--	4 (3.42)	--	--	--	--	117 (100.0)
Self-employment in skilled activity	--	--	26 (81.25)	--	6 (18.75)	--	--	32 (100.00)
Self-employment in artisanal/ handicraft/ household activity	--	--	12 (100.0)	--	--	--	--	12 (100.0)
Self-employment in trade/business	2 (11.11)	3 (16.66)	13 (72.23)	--	--	--	--	18 (100.0)
Self-employment in service activity	--	--	--	--	--	--	--	--
Manufacturing activity	--	--	--	--	--	--	--	--
Export	--	--	--	--	--	--	--	--
Seasonal activity	--	--	1 (100.0)	--	--	--	--	1 (100.0)
Total	115 (63.88)	3 (1.66)	56 (31.12)	--	6 (3.34)	--	--	180 (100.0)

Note: Figures under bracket denote per cent to horizontal total.

Source: Based on the information collected from the field.

artisanal/handicraft/handloom/household activities, self-employment in trade/business and under seasonal activity. Loans and subsidies have been primarily given by DRDA and Banks, whereas, employment has been generated mainly by the Gram Sabha and DRDA.

In urban areas, a majority of minority household members has received loans and subsidies by banks under self-employment generating skill intensive activities. Same is found true under self-employment in artisanal/handicraft/handloom/house-hold activities and self-employment in trade/business activities. In the district, the employment for a majority of minority household members has been generated under employment generating programme through Gram Sabha and DRDA. Also, a majority of minority household members has received loans and subsidies mainly from the banks and DRDA.

1. Financial Assistance, Employment and Income Generation

Table V.15 provides financial assistance provided to the members of minority households and the average employment and income generated there from. In rural areas, the financial assistance per person under different programmes and schemes has been worked out to be Rs.12,462.00, which has varied from Rs.15,000.00 in seasonal activity to Rs.12,223.00 in self-employed trade/business.

In rural areas, the employment per person comes to about 43 days from all programmes/schemes, being highest in self-employed, trade/business and seasonal activities (150 days), while lowest in employment generating schemes (33 days). Income per person generated through all programmes/schemes is worked out to be Rs.2,454.00, being highest in self-employed in trade/business (Rs.9,445.00), while lowest in employment generating programmes/schemes (Rs.1707.00).

TABLE V.15

Financial Assistance, Employment and Income Generation Per Person From Different Development Programmes/Schemes in Rural and Urban Areas: Rampur: 1997

Area / Programmes / Schemes	*Financial assistance per person (Rs.)*	*Employment generated per person (days)*	*Income generated per person (Rs.)*
Rural			
Employment generating programme/schemes	- -	33.39	1,707.00
Self-employment in skilled activity	- -	- -	- -
Self-employment in artisanal/handicraft/ household activity	12,334.00	60.00	7,668.00
Self-employment in trade/business	12,223.00	150.00	9,445.00
Self-employment in service activity	- -	- -	- -
Manufacturing activity	- -	- -	- -
Export	- -	- -	- -
Seasonal activity	15,000.00	150.00	6,000.00
Sub-Total	**12,462.00**	**42.70**	**2,454.00**

Table V.15 (contd..)

Area / Programmes / Schemes	*Financial assistance per person (Rs.)*	*Employment generated per person (days)*	*Income generated per person (Rs.)*
Urban			
Employment generating programme/schemes	- -	60.00	3,714.00
Self-employment in skilled activity	13,00.00	180.00	9,688.00
Self-employment in artisanal/ handicraft/household activity	15,334.00	180.00	10,000.00
Self-employment in trade/business	15,778.00	270.00	10,000.00
Self-employment in service activity	- -	- -	- -
Manufacturing activity	- -	- -	- -
Export	- -	- -	- -
Seasonal activity	- -	- -	- -
Sub-Total	**13,920.00**	**179.60**	**9,063.00**
Distict			
Employment generating programme	- -	34.98	1,828.00
Self-employment in skilled activity	13,000.00	180.00	9,688.00
Self-employment in artisanal/ handicraft/household activity	14,584.00	163.63	9,417.00
Self-employment in trade/business	14,000.00	210.00	9,723.00
Self-employment in service activity	- -	- -	- -
Manufacturing activity	- -	- -	- -
Export	- -	- -	- -
Seasonal activity	15,000.00	150.00	6,000.00
Total	**13,619.00**	**86.57**	**4,543.00**

Source: Based on the information collected from the field.

In urban areas, the financial assistance received by minority household members from all development programmes/schemes comes to Rs.13,920.0 per person. Of which, highest is from self-employment in trade/business (Rs.15,778.00) per person, while lowest from self-employed in skilled activity (Rs.13,000.00) per person. The average employment generated from all the development programmes comes to about 180 days per person. The income generated from all development programmes comes to Rs.9,063.00 per person. It varies from one development programme to another. Whereas, highest is from self-employed in trade/business and self-employed artisanal/handicraft/handloom/household activity (Rs.10,000 per person from each activity), whereas, the lowest is from employment generating programmes/schemes (Rs.3,714.00 per person).

In the district, the value of financial assistance per person comes to Rs.13,619.00 and employment to about 87 days per person. The income generated from these programmes comes to Rs.4,543.00 per person. Employment generated per person is found highest from self-employed trade/business (210 days), while lowest from employment generating programmes/schemes (about 35 days). Income generated is found to be highest from self-employed trade/business (Rs.9,723.00) per person, whereas, lowest from employment generating programmes/schemes (Rs.1,828.00) per person.

2. Steps Required for Development of Minorities

We have also asked relevant questions from minority households on steps required for their development. Multiple responses of the minority households have been recorded in Table V.16. Responses pertain to the development of minorities at village, city and at the district level. In rural areas, a majority of minority households feels that there is a need for reservation of jobs for minorities in all government

TABLE V.16

Responses* of Minority Households on Steps Required for their Development in Rural and Urban Areas: Rampur, 1997

Steps required to be undertaken	*Rural households feeling for development at:*			*Urban households feeling for development at:*			*Total*		
	Village level (No.)	*City level (No.)*	*District level (No.)*	*Village level (No.)*	*City level (No.)*	*District level (No.)*	*At village level (No.)*	*At city level (No.)*	*At district level (No.)*
Free education	85 (26.07)	64 (19.63)	84 (25.77)	27 (15.52)	30 (17.24)	36 (20.69)	112 (22.40)	94 (18.80)	120 (24.00)
Effective utilization of welfare schemes	41 (15.58)	42 (12.88)	42 (12.88)	34 (19.54)	105 (60.34)	39 (22.41)	75 (15.00)	147 (29.40)	81 (16.20)
Development of cottage industries on priority basis	79 (24.23)	43 (13.19)	41 (12.54)	23 (18.39)	74 (42.52)	14 (8.05)	102 (20.40)	117 (23.40)	55 (11.00)
Awareness about the welfare schemes of Government	67 (20.55)	56 (17.18)	70 (21.47)	55 (31.61)	28 (16.09)	16 (9.19)	122 (24.40)	84 (16.80)	86 (17.20)
Reservation of minorities in all the Govt. services	105 (32.21)	105 (32.21)	184 (56.44)	45 (25.86)	91 (52.30)	105 (60.34)	150 (30.00)	196 (39.20)	289 (57.80)
Representation in all the development works	93 (28.53)	32 (9.82)	55 (16.87)	23 (13.22)	-- --	--	116 (23.20)	32 (6.40)	55 (11.00)

Steps required to be undertaken	*Rural households feeling for development at:*			*Urban households feeling for development at:*			*Total*		
	Village level (No.)	*City level (No.)*	*District level (No.)*	*Village level (No.)*	*City level (No.)*	*District level (No.)*	*At village level (No.)*	*At city level (No.)*	*At district level (No.)*
Emphasis on fisheries	73 (22.39)	--	--	7 (4.02)	--	--	80 (16.00)	--	--
Emphasis on poultry	65 (19.94)	--	--	5 (2.87)	--	--	70 (14.00)	--	--
Fundamental facilities for cottage industries	35 (10.74)	--	--	5 (2.87)	--	--	40 (8.00)	--	--
N=	326 (100.00)	326 (100.00)	326 (100.00)	174 (100.00)	174 (100.00)	174 (100.00)	500 (100.00)	500 (100.00)	500 (100.00)

* Indicates multiple responses.
Note: Figures within parentheses denote per cent to vertical total.
Source: Based on the information collected from the field.

jobs (32.21 per cent) followed by the representation in all development works (28.53 per cent) and free education facility (26.07 per cent) at the village level.

In urban areas, a majority of minority households feels that there is need for reservation of minorities in all government services at the city level. Also, a majority of them (31.61 per cent) is of the view that awareness about the welfare schemes of the government needs to be carried out at the village level followed by effective utilization of welfare schemes at the city level (60.34 per cent). The reservation of minorities in all government services is also required to be made at the district level for the development of minorities.

In the district, a majority of minority households feels that there is a need of reservation for minorities in all government services at village, city and at the district level on priority basis (Table V.16). It is, however, important to note that a majority of minority households in rural, urban and in the district is found unaware about the coaching facilities available for the competitive examinations (Table V.17).

TABLE V.17

Awareness about Coaching Facilities by the Minority Households for Competitive Examinations in Rural and Urban Areas : Rampur, 1997

Area	*Awareness*		
	Yes (No.)	*No (No.)*	*Total (No.)*
Rural	33(10.12)	293(89.88)	326(100.0)
Urban	52(29.89)	122(70.11)	174(100.0)
Total	85(17.00)	415(83.00)	500(100.0)

Note: Figures within parentheses denote per cent to horizontal total.

Source: Based on the information collected from the field.

Factors Affecting Growth of Entrepreneurship

We have also examined the role of factors affecting the growth of entrepreneurship of minorities engaged in manufacturing activities and also to those who worked as artisan and self-employed. Table V.18 provides multiple responses on these counts. In urban manufacturing, a majority of minority households has expressed (i) the shortage of finance, (ii) competition with larger units/ entrepreneurs and (iii) lack of awareness about the government's welfare schemes as a major obstacles of growth of entrepreneurship. A similar finding, to a large extent, has also been found at the district level. In rural artisonal activities, one-half of minority households have expressed the (i) lack of initiative, (ii) lack of knowledge, (iii) limited scope/market for the product/services, (iv) lack of managerial skills and (v) lack of training facility for skill development as major constraints for the growth of entrepreneurship.

In urban areas, such factors include : (i) shortage of finance, (ii) absence of institutional support, (iii) non-availability of organization to protect wages/exploitations of artisans; (iv) lack of awareness about the development programmes/schemes of the government and (v) inadequate institutional support for marketing of products/services. In the district, the main factors affecting the growth of entrepreneurship are : (i) non-availability of institutions/ organizations to protect wages and exploitation, (ii) inadequate institutional support for the marketing of products/services and (iii) shortage of finance.

With regard to self-employed activities, the main factors in rural areas are : (i) shortage of finance and (ii) lack of awareness about the development programmes/ schemes of the government. In urban areas, factors affecting the growth of entrepreneurship for the minority households include: (i) shortage of finance, (ii) lack of awareness about development programmes/schemes of the government, (iii)

TABLE V.18

Responses* of Minority Households on Factors Affecting the Growth of Entrepreneurship in Important Economic Activities in Rural and Urban Areas: Rampur, 1997

Factors affecting entrepreneurship	*Economic activities of the minority households and area*								
	Manufacturing			*Artisanal activities*			*Self-employed activities*		
	Rural (No.)	*Urban (No.)*	*Total (No.)*	*Rural (No.)*	*Urban (No.)*	*Total (No.)*	*Rural (No.)*	*Urban (No.)*	*Total (No.)*
Lack of initiative	--	--	--	4(50.00)	1(6.25)	5(20.83)	3(12.00)	2(3.70)	5(6.33)
Lack of knowledge	--	1(5.56)	1(5.56)	4(50.00)	--	4(16.67)	5(20.00)	3(5.56)	8(10.13)
Shortage of finance	--	7(38.89)	7(38.89)	2(25.00)	9(56.25)	11(45.83)	12(48.00)	33(61.11)	45(56.96)
Limited scope/market for the product/service	--	1(5.56)	1(5.56)	4(50.00)	--	4(16.67)	4(16.00)	--	4(5.06)
Tough competition with larger units/ entrepreneurs	--	6(33.33)	6(33.33)	3(37.50)	3(18.75)	6(25.00)	6(24.00)	20(37.04)	26(32.91)
Lack of managerial skills	--	--	--	4(50.00)	2(12.50)	6(25.00)	2(8.00)	7(12.96)	9(11.39)
Shortage of skilled workers	--	1(5.56)	1(5.56)	2(25.00)	1(6.25)	3(12.00)	3(12.00)	16(29.63)	19(24.05)
Lack of training facility in skill development	--	1(5.56)	1(5.56)	4(50.00)	--	4(16.67)	2(8.00)	3(5.56)	5(6.33)
Lack of awareness about development programmes/schemes of the Government	--	6(33.33)	6(33.33)	2(25.00)	7(43.75)	9(37.50)	11(44.00)	22(40.74)	33(41.77)

Factors affecting entrepreneurship	Economic activities of the minority households and area								
	Manufacturing			Artisanal activities			Self-employed activities		
	Rural (No.)	Urban (No.)	Total (No.)	Rural (No.)	Urban (No.)	Total (No.)	Rural (No.)	Urban (No.)	Total (No.)
Lack of institutional support for marketing of products/services	- -	5(27.78)	5(27.78)	4(50.00)	7(43.75)	11(95.83)	2(8.00)	6(11.11)	8(10.13)
Absence of institution/organization to protect wages/exploitation of artisans	- -	3(6.47)	3(6.47)	2(25.00)	10(55.56)	12(50.00)	- -	3(5.56)	3(3.80)
N=	- -	18(100.0)	18(100.0)	8(100.0)	16(100.0)	24(100.0)	25(100.0)	54(100.0)	79(100.0)

* Indicates multiple responses.

N= Number of households in rural, urban and in the district.

Note: Figures within parentheses denote percent to figure 'N'.

Source: Based on the information collected from the field.

fierce competition with large unit/entrepreneurs and (iv) shortage of skilled workers. In the district, the principal factors affecting the growth of entrepreneurship include : (i) shortage of finance, (ii) lack of awareness about the development programmes/schemes of the government and (iii) the tough competition with large unit/entrepreneurs.

Common Community Assets

We have also examined various aspects of common community assets from the households of minority community. Table V.19 provides information on awareness about common community assets. A majority of minority households is found aware about the common community assets. A majority of minority households in rural (87.12 per cent), urban (66.09 per cent) and in the district (79.80 per cent) is found aware about the common community assets.

TABLE V.19

Responses of Minority Households about Awareness of Common Community Assets in Rural and Urban Areas: Rampur, 1997

Area	*Response*		
	Yes (No.)	*No (No.)*	*Total (No.)*
Rural	284(87.12)	42(12.88)	326(100.0)
Urban	115(66.09)	59(33.91)	174(100.0)
Total	399(66.09)	101(20.20)	500(100.0)

Note: Figures within parentheses denote per cent to horizontal total.
Source: Based on the information collected from the field.

We have also examined in Table V.20 the purposes for which common community assets are used. In rural, urban and in the district, the place of worship as a part of common community assets is found exclusively used for the worshipping, open field for playing and meadow. A part of it is also utilized illegally by few minority households.

TABLE V.20

Responses* of Minority Households on Purpose-wise Utilization of Common Community Assets in Rural and Urban Areas: Rampur, 1997

Area / Particulars	*Purpose-wise utilization of common community assets*							
	Worshiping (No.)	*Playing (No.)*	*Used as meadow (No.)*	*Illegal possession (No.)*	*Schooling the children (No.)*	*Studying (No.)*	*Playing & other extra curricular (No.)*	*(N=)*
Rural								
Worship place	278(97.88)	--	--	--	--	--	--	284(100.00)
Open field	--	71(25.00)	68(23.94)	43(15.14)	--	--	--	284(100.00)
Madarasa	--	--	--	--	16(5.63)	--	--	284(100.00)
Library	--	--	--	--	--	--	--	--
Park	--	--	--	--	--	--	--	--
Urban								
Worship place	115(100.0)	--	--	--	--	--	--	115(100.00)
Open field	--	18(15.65)	16(13.91)	--	--	--	--	115(100.00)
Madarasa	--	--	--	--	67(58.26)	--	--	115(100.00)
Library	--	--	--	--	--	23(20.00)	--	115(100.00)
Park	--	--	--	--	--	--	7(6.08)	115(100.00)

Area / Particulars	Purpose-wise utilization of common community assets							
	Worshiping (No.)	Playing (No.)	Used as meadow (No.)	Illegal possession (No.)	Schooling the children (No.)	Studying (No.)	Playing & other extra.curricular (No.)	(N=)
District								
Worship place	393(98.50)	--	--	--	--	--	--	399(100.00)
Open field	--	89(22.31)	84(21.05)	43(10.78)	--	--	--	399(100.00)
Madarasa	--	--	--	--	83(20.80)	--	--	399(100.00)
Library	--	--	--	--	--	23(5.76)	--	399(100.00)
Park	--	--	--	--	--	--	7(1.75)	399(100.00)

* Indicates multiple responses.

Note: Figures under bracket indicate per cent to figure 'N'.

Madarsa is used exclusively for studying by the children, library is used for studying and park for play ground.

Household's View for the Development of Minorities

We may now discuss the steps required for the development of minorities based on the responses collected from the minority households. This is given in Table V.21. In rural areas, a majority of minority households (36.80 per cent) has expressed the need for free education with scholarship for educational development. Next to this comes the introduction of technical and employment oriented education followed by establishment of higher educational institutions in villages as for each over 32 per cent of minority households have felt these requirements.

TABLE V.21

Responses* of Minority Households for their Socio-Economic Development in Rural and Urban Areas: Rampur, 1997

Heads of development / Steps required	*Responses of Minority households in:*		
	Rural (No.)	*Urban (No.)*	*Total (No.)*
A. Educational Development			
Technical and employment oriented education	107(32.82)	61(35.05)	168(33.60)
Free education with scholarship	120(36.80)	92(52.87)	212(42.40)
Awareness about the education	89(27.30)	38(21.83)	127(25.40)
Establishment of higher educational institutions in villages	105(32.20)	--	105(21.00)
Emphasis on girls' education	46(14.11)	72(41.37)	118(30.60)
Proper arrangement of teachers	52(15.95)	20(11.49(	72(14.40)
Arrangement of Urdu teachers	69(21.16)	53(30.45)	122(24.40)
B. Economic Development			
Financial support for self-employment	190(58.28)	61(35.05)	251(50.20)
Emphasis on cottage industries	140(42.94)	60(34.48)	200(40.00)
Awareness for self-employment generating programmes/schemes	101(30.98)	52(29.88)	153(30.60)
Emphasis on fisheries, poultry and others	37(11.34)	16(9.19)	53(10.60)
Fundamental facilities for cottage industries	22(6.74)	24(13.79)	46(9.20)

C. Health Improvement			
Free medicine facilities	146(44.78)	92(52.87)	238(47.60)
Women hospitals with women doctors	110(33.74)	30(17.24)	140(28.00)
Primary health centers in he villages	168(51.53)	--	168(33.60)
Awareness about the family planning programmes	63(19.32)	63(36.20)	126(25.20)
Prohibition on illicit drugs	54(16.56)	21(12.06)	75(15.00)
D. Improving Housing and Sanitary Conditions			
Housing for weaker sections	157(48.15)	65(37.35)	222(44.40)
Roads and drainage facility at Panchayat level	127(38.95)	79(45.40)	206(41.20)
Proper arrangement of drinking water	91(27.91)	26(14.94)	117(23.40)
Appointment of sweepers	66(20.24)	28(16.09)	94(18.80)
Availability of land for housing	31(9.50)	24(13.79)	55(11.00)
Interest free loan for housing	66(20.24)	26(14.94)	92(18.40)
Construction of latrines	53(16.25)	34(19.54)	87(17.40)
E. Effective Utilization of Welfare Schemes of Government			
Planning at grass root level	137(42.02)	28(16.09)	165(33.00)
Proper publicity	142(43.55)	81(46.55)	223(44.60)
Benefit to needy people	123(37.73)	59(33.90)	182(36.40)
Time to time inspection	66(20.24)	33(18.96)	99(19.80)
F. Productive Use of Manpower Resources			
Technical training	151(46.31)	58(33.33)	209(41.80)
Financial support for self-employment	69(21.16)	49(28.16)	118(23.60)
Loan at low rate of interest	69(21.16)	44(25.28)	113(22.60)
Government sponsored scheme for employment	82(25.15)	28(16.09)	110(22.00)
Assurance for job	83(25.46)	25(14.36)	108(21.60)
N =	326(100.0)	174(100.0)	500(100.00)

* Indicates multiple responses.

N = Indicates total number of minority households in rural, urban and in the district.

Note: Figures under bracket denote percent to figure 'N'.

Source: Based on the information collected from the field.

In urban areas, free education with scholarship and girls' education have been expressed as pressing need for educational development. In the district, free education with scholarship, technical and employment oriented education and girls education have been considered principal needs for educational development for minorities.

In rural, urban and in the district, financial support

for self-employment and development of cottage industries have been emphasized for economic development. For health development, a majority of rural minority households has emphasized the need for PHC in villages followed by free medicine facilities. In the urban and in the district, free medicine facility followed by awareness about the family planning programme and schemes have been emphasized.

Further, with a view to improve the housing and sanitary condition, a majority of minority households in the rural areas feels that houses need to be given to weaker sections along with roads and drainage facility at the panchayat level. In urban areas, provision of housing to weaker section along with roads and drainage facility has been felt. In the district, provision for housing for weaker sections followed by roads, drainage at the panchayat level has been felt.

With regard to effective utilization of welfare schemes of the government, a proper publicity followed by planning at the grass-root level is felt by the majority of minority households in rural areas. In urban areas and in Rampur district, a proper publicity and provision of benefits to the needy people have been felt.

As for the productive use of manpower resources, a majority of rural minority households has felt the support of technical training and assurance for jobs. In the urban areas, a majority of households has required technical training followed by financial support for self-employment. In the district, a majority of households has felt technical training as their primary requirement. It emerges that free education with scholarship for educational development, financial support for self-employment for economic development, free medicine facilities for health improvement, provision of housing for weaker section for improving housing and sanitary conditions, proper publicity for effective utilization of welfare schemes of the government and technical training for productive use of manpower resources are the important factors for the development of minorities.

Summing-Up

A majority of minority population in rural areas is found employed as self-employed, while in urban, they are engaged as skilled workers. In the district, a majority of minority population is found engaged as skilled workers. Dissatisfaction across different economic activities among minority community has, however, prevailed. A low market demand and irregular earnings to artisans, exploitation by middlemen and irregular earnings for skilled workers and financial constraint for self-employed have emerged as principal reasons for dissatisfaction among minority population.

A majority of minority population wishes to start general store, cloth selling, pan selling, tea stall, atta chakki and cycle repairing activities. To start a new activity in rural areas requires Rs.32,755 per person. In urban area, bidi making, zari works, rickshaw pulling, T.V., Radio repairing and motor binding are found principal economic activities. The new economic activities proposed are : general store, tea stall, motor binding and cycle repairing and parts shop. To start an economic activity requires Rs.22,026 per person.

In the district, to start a new activity requires Rs.29,787 per person. Also, proposed economic activities, such as, general store, selling of cloth, selling of pan, atta chakki, cycle repairing and tea stalls are found advantageous in terms of employment and income generation and marketing in rural areas. In urban areas, tea stalls and hotels have been found advantageous economic activities. In the district, the advantageous economic activities include : general store, cloth selling, tea stalls and hotel.

Training has been emphasized to enhance the skill

development and that for entrepreneurship/management in urban areas explicitly. So as to improve the economic condition of un-employed youth, a need for finance and training has been felt. Across different economic activities, self-employed rural youths have felt the need for educational skills in zari work, tailoring and in repairing, while urban self-employed youths in zari work, repairing and blacksmithy. Similarly, under-employed youths in rural areas have felt the need for finance, fertilizers and seeds to improve their economic conditions, while those in urban areas finance, awareness about self-employment generating schemes and training have been felt.

As far the benefit from rural development programmes, a majority of minority households in rural and in urban has felt that such programmes and schemes are not beneficial for improving their economic conditions. Across different programmes/schemes, it has, however, been discovered that Total Literacy Campaign, Computer Education under skill development and Non-Formal Education have been found to be considerably beneficial in rural areas. In urban areas, Literacy Campaign and Coaching Facility for Competitive Examinations have been found beneficial. However, development programmes are found more beneficial in rural than that in urban areas. In rural areas, financial requirements in terms of loans and subsidies have been provided by DRDA and banks to members of minority households to create employment and self-employment in artisanal/handicraft/handloom/ household activities through Gram Sabhas.

In urban areas, loans and subsidies have generally been given by banks, which have generated the employment in artisanal/handicraft/handloom/ household and in trade and business activities. The employment generation from all economic activities has been worked out to about 43 days per person in rural, 180 days in urban areas. In district, it is found to be about 87 days per person. Financial assistance is worked out to be Rs.12,462 per person in rural and to Rs.13,920 per person in the urban areas. It comes to Rs.13,619 per person in the Rampur district. Income generated comes to Rs.2,454 per person in rural, Rs.9,063 in urban and to Rs.4,543 in the district.

Growth of entrepreneurship has mainly been affected adversely by the inadequate finance, lack of awareness about the development programmes/schemes of the government and severe competition with large units/ entrepreneurs. Common community assets, such as, place of worship is found used exclusively for worshipping, open field for playing, madarsa for studying in rural and in urban areas. In urban areas, library is found used for studying and park for playing.

Study also examines the views of minority households for their development. In rural and urban areas, a majority of minority households feels that educational level of their children can be enhanced by providing free education with scholarship. In the district, free education with scholarship, technical and employment generating education and girl's education have been emphasized. As for economic development, financial support and development of cottage industries have been emphasized in rural, urban and in the district. For health improvement, opening up of PHC in villages and free medicine facility in rural, free medicine facility and awareness about family planning programmes in urban and in the district have been felt by a majority of minority households. For improving the housing and sanitary condition, housing along with roads and drainage to weaker sections has been emphasized in rural, urban and in the district. For effective utilization of welfare schemes, a majority of community households feels that it may be enhanced if publicity and planning are undertaken at the grassroot level in rural, urban and in the district. It is also found that use of manpower resources can be made more effective by providing technical training to the minorities.

6

General Summary, Conclusions and Policy Recommendations

We may now summarise the general findings and draw some conclusions arising out of the present study. This is done with the hope that it will not only sharpen our understanding about the socio-economic aspects of minorities but also help in exploring certain policy recommendations for the socio-economic development of minorities in the Rampur district.

It has generally been recognized that a majority of minority population in rural areas is engaged as labour, small and marginal farmers, artisans or self-employed in the small scale trade, while those in urban areas are employed in traditional industries, such as, handloom, powerloom, block making, wood carving, metal work, carpet weaving, perfumery, leather work, glass work, textile printing and other handicrafts, such as, embroidery, chikan, zari, etc. Also, many of them are engaged in transport, manufacturing and exporting. The remaining is seen dependent on salaried jobs in the government, public and private sector organizations or in self-employed service sector economic activities.

It may be recapitulated that a majority of minority population in rural and those in urban areas engaged in various economic activities is rarely satisfied. This is inter-alia due to long and strenuous working hours, low wages and profit margins. Added to these, their working conditions and living environment are extremely hazardous for their health. Besides, illiteracy has led to educational backwardness, while unemployment to high poverty, high infant mortality and morbidity. Thus, owing to poor economic and living conditions, use of non-potable water, illiteracy and unhygienic and insanitary environment, a large proportion of minorities suffer from poor health conditions. These have affected adversely the maternal and child health. In response to these, mortality rates among infants and toddlers are significantly higher among minorities, which are consequences of various ailments, such as, tuberculosis, eye ailments and other types of diseases. Further, self-employed and under-employed youths from minorities do not generally have the man and material resources required to improve their socioeconomic conditions.

It may be noted that there exists various developmental programmes for socio-economic development of poor, such as, Integrated Rural Development Programme (IRDP), Drought Prone Area Programme (DPAP), Jawahar Rozgar Yojana (JRY), Training of Rural Youth for Self-Employment Programme (TRYSEM), Total Literacy Campaign (TLC), Immunization Campaign, Nehru Yuva Kendras, etc., besides number of programmes and activities pursued from time to time by the government and NGOs. These developmental programmes have inbuilt structural constraints due to which benefits from these have not generally percolated from top to down level. Therefore, for the speedy socio-economic development of minorities, there is a pressing need to approach the problem from population end. Thus, 'area based approach' rather than 'programme end' approach needs to be followed. Present study towards this direction examines the various socio-economic aspects of 500 households belonging to minorities spread over in rural and in urban areas in Rampur district.

Social Characteristics of Minorities

So as to follow the 'area based approach' for the socio-economic development of minorities, it is essential to understand in-depth the social characteristics of minorities. Chapter II, of the study, examines various social characteristics of minorities. In rural areas, 78.83 per cent of minority households are found from general, while to 21.17 per cent from the backward caste community. However, there are intra-block variations of minority households by castes. In Swar block, general caste consists of 87.25 per cent, while backward caste to 12.75 per cent. In Bilaspur block, 64.75 per cent of minority households are from general, while to 35.25 per cent are from the backward caste category.

In urban areas, 63.22 per cent of minority households belong to general, while to 36.78 per cent are from the backward caste. Intra-city variations have also persisted. In Rampur city, 70.45 per cent of minority households are from general, while to 29.55 per cent are from the backward caste category. In Swar city, 40.48 per cent of minority households are from general, while to 59.22 per cent belong to backward caste category. In the district, 73.40 per cent of minority households are from general, while to 26.60 per cent are from backward caste category. Thus, finding of the study suggests that general caste is relatively more significant than to that of backward caste among the minority households.

A majority of the family members of minorities in rural as well as in urban areas are found youngsters. They are 40.20 per cent in rural and to 33.78 per cent in urban areas. These belong within the age group of <15 years. In rural and urban total, minority population to <15 years of age is found to be 37.97 per cent. However, between rural and urban, young minority population is found relatively more significant in the former (40.20 per cent) than to that in the later (33.78 per cent). Thus, non-adult population has been found to be relatively more significant than to those of adult population.

Since non-adult population from minority community has dominated, a majority of them are found to be unmarried. This is found true in case of males and females in rural, urban and in the district. Between rural and urban, unmarried males are found to be relatively more significant in urban (63.55 per cent) than to those in rural (60.99 per cent). A similar finding also emerges in the case of unmarried females. The unmarried female population is found to be 55.31 per cent in urban, which is higher than to those in rural areas of 48.90 per cent. In the district, unmarried males are found to be 61.85 per cent, while to that of females to 51.22 per cent. Size of household is worked out to be 5.97 for the district, which is composed of 5.98 for the rural and to 5.95 for the urban areas. Thus, size of household is found to be marginally larger in rural than to that in urban areas.

Education has unquestionably been recognized as an important contributory factor for the socio-economic development. In view of this, study examines the level of education of minority population. Finding suggests that a majority of minority population has acquired education up to primary level in rural, urban and in the district. The minority household members with primary level of education are found to be 31.78 per cent in rural, 28.67 per cent in urban and to30.70 per cent in the district. Minority members beyond the primary level of education are found to be larger in urban than that in rural areas. It is, however, dissatisfying that illiteracy has prevailed considerably in rural, urban and in the district. For instance, over 56 per cent of minority population in rural, around 52 per cent in urban and to about 55 per cent in the district are found illiterates.

As a majority of minority population is illiterate, the

analysis has further been extended to look into the enrolment, non-enrolment and drop-outs. In rural areas, enrolment for males and females has sharply declined with the increase in the age of the corresponding minority children. In sharp contrast to above, non-enrolment and drop-outs have increased generally with the increase in the age of minority male and female children. Of the total rural minority male children, 57.98 per cent of them are found enrolled, 27.47 per cent never enrolled and to 14.55 per cent to drop outs. Similarly, of the total rural minority female children, 41.72 per cent are found enrolled, 49.69 per cent never enrolled and to 8.59 per cent drop outs. Of the total of minority children (males and females), 51.52 per cent are found enrolled, 36.30 per cent never enrolled and to 12.18 per cent drop outs. Government school is found as the principal centre for learning for minority children. For male students, private school has turned out to be more important than madarsa, while for female, the later is found more important than the former.

More or less, a similar finding has also emerged in the case of urban areas, where enrolment has deteriorated sharply for minority children (males and females), whereas, that of non-enrolment and drop outs have increased with the increase in the age of the minority children. Out of urban male children, 61.29 per cent are found enrolled, 25.67 per cent never enrolled and to 13.04 per cent drop outs. Of the urban female children, 46.07 per cent are found enrolled, 41.95 per cent never enrolled and to 11.98 per cent are drop outs. Of the total urban children (males and females), 54.77 per cent are found enrolled, 32.64 per cent never enrolled and to 12.59 per cent drop outs. Between urban males and females, non-enrolment is found higher in case of females than that of males, while vice-versa is found true for enrolment and drop outs. Government school again emerges as primary centre for education for minority male and female students. Private school and madarsa have emerged next, in order of importance, as centre for learning.

Drop out in rural areas, has mainly been found after the Class Vth, which comes to 33.34 per cent for males, 35.71 per cent for females and to 34 per cent for male and female total. A similar is also the case for urban areas, where 23.81 per cent of males, 38.89 per cent of females and to 33.33 per cent of both (males and females) have dropped out after the Class Vth. In the district, 31.18 per cent of males, 37.50 per cent of females and to 33.76 per cent of both (males and females) have dropped out after the Class Vth Standard of education. A majority of minority households, 88.34 per cent in rural and to 84.48 per cent in urban feels that the enrolment of minority children is low. This is primarily due to the poor economic conditions of minority households followed by consideration of study of Quran and Theology.

Economic Characteristics of Minorities

So as to understand the level of economic development of minority community, it would be useful to look into the various economic characteristics of minorities. This has been examined in Chapter III, of the present study. General findings suggest that a majority of minority households i.e., 49.69 per cent in rural areas is engaged in farming, while 33.33 per cent in urban areas in business/trade. In rural and urban total, a majority of minority households (38.60 per cent) is found employed as wage earners. The finding, thus, underlines the farming in rural, business/trade in urban and hired labour-intensive occupation in the district as a principal absorber of workforce from minority community.

Analysis has also been extended to understand in-depth the significance of economic activities at a more level of disaggregation as the absorber of the minority household members. Household work turns out to be the primary economic occupation, which has employed to 30.54 per cent of minority population in rural, 31.37 per cent in urban and to 30.83 per cent in the district. In rural areas, income per household is worked out to be Rs.14,830.67 per annum and per capita to Rs.2,533.96, which is found higher than those in urban areas of Rs.14,240.23 per household and to Rs.2,391.70 per capita. In the district the corresponding figure comes to Rs.14,625.20 and to Rs.2,483.90 respectively.

The income in rural areas has mainly been generated from business, service, artisanal work, etc. (50.63 per cent) followed by agriculture (43.37 per cent), while that in urban areas mainly by business, service, artisanal work, etc. (91.57 per cent). In the district, income has been generated mainly by business, service, artisanal work, etc. (64.50 per cent) followed by agriculture (30.07 per cent). Thus, business, service, artisanal work, etc. followed by agriculture have been discovered as the main sources of income generation in rural and in the district, while business, service, artisanal work, etc. in urban areas. High productivity of land seems to be an important explanatory factor inter-alia for income generation in rural areas and in the district.

We have also examined poverty profile of minority households. Following IRDP poverty norm of 1994, 108 households (or 33.13 per cent) in rural; 60 households (or 34.48 per cent) in urban; and to 168 households (or 33.60 per cent) in the district are found living below the poverty line. Thus, poverty is found marginally higher in urban than that to in rural, but lower in urban than that in the district as a whole.

As for financial linkages, out of 326, 28.53 per cent of households in rural areas have taken loan. Loans have mainly been taken from commercial and non-commercial banks (46.24 per cent), money lenders (19.35 per cent), relatives and friends (15.05 per cent) and other government departments (10.75 per cent). In the urban areas, out of 174, 16.67 per cent of minority households have taken loan. Loans have mainly flowed from commercial and non-commercial banks (51.73 per cent), relatives and friends (17.24 per cent), traders (13.79 per cent), money lenders (10.34 per cent), etc. In the district, out of 500, 24.40 per cent of households have taken loan. Loan has mainly been taken from commercial and non-commercial banks (47.54 per cent), money lenders (17.21 per cent), relatives and friends (15.57 per cent), etc. It emerges that commercial and non-commercial banks are the major lending source for the majority of borrowers in rural, urban and in the district.

A majority of minority households in rural, has taken loan for the agricultural work, especially to purchase fertilizers and agricultural instruments (43.02 per cent) and to start business and/or its expansion (22.58 per cent). In urban areas, a majority of minority households has taken loan for business and its expansion (68.96 per cent), house construction (10.34 per cent), etc. In the district, a majority of households (33.61 per cent) has taken loan each for (i) agricultural work/purchase of fertilizers/ instruments and (ii) business and its expansion in equal proportion. Thus, loan has mainly been taken for agricultural work and for business and its expansion. Another dimension is the repayment of loan by the minority households. The amount of loan refunded to loan taken is found higher in urban areas (59.39 per cent) than that in rural areas (42.20 per cent) and in the district (46.71 per cent).

Housing Characteristics and Health Conditions of Minorities

Another important dimension is to examine the housing characteristics and health conditions of minority community, which has been attempted in Chapter IV, of the present study. The general findings suggest that a majority of houses is ancestral in rural (57.06 per cent), urban (63.22

per cent) and in the district (59.20 per cent). Also, kutcha houses are found to be relatively more significant in rural (36.20 per cent), pucca in urban (41.95 per cent) and semi-kutcha in the district (37.20 per cent). Similarly, houses with two rooms accommodation are found to be relatively more significant in rural (42.02 per cent), urban (50.57 per cent) and in the district (45 per cent). A majority of houses in rural (90.49 per cent), urban (64.37 per cent) and in the district (81.40 per cent) is found without separate kitchen facility. Service based toilet facility is found in common use in rural (57.66 per cent), urban (71.27 per cent) and in the district (62.40 per cent). Garbage has generally been disposed off nearby the house in rural, away from the house in urban and nearby the house in the district. Water is found open and running in rural, urban and in the district. Hand pumps owned either by government or by individual households in rural, urban and in the district are found as the main source of water for drinking. Oil lamp/lantern as source of lighting is found more significant in rural, electricity in urban and oil lamp/lantern in the district. Firewood is found used commonly by the majority of minority households in rural, urban and in the district as fuel for cooking.

We have also examined as to whether or not minority households are satisfied in relation to health conditions of their family members. As much as 73 per cent of households in rural, 71 per cent in urban and to 72 per cent in the district have been found satisfied. The dissatisfied households are found to be 27 per cent in rural, 29 per cent in urban and to 28 per cent in the district. A majority of dissatisfied members of minority households has suffered from respiratory problem in rural (29.35 per cent), urban (43.14 per cent) and in the district (34.27 per cent) and a majority of them in rural (32.43 per cent), urban (46.67 per cent) and in the district (36.54 per cent) has been found suffering to more than 3 years.

Monthly expenditure on medical treatment per patient for respiratory has been worked out to be Rs.141.11 in rural, Rs.123.86 in urban and to Rs.133.36 in the district. Monthly expenditure incurred on medical treatment per patient for all diseases has been found to be Rs.177.50 in rural, Rs.149.12 in urban and to Rs.167.38 in the district. Besides respiratory, other important diseases include : stomach, bone and joint problems and tuberculosis in rural, stomach, tuberculosis and heart problem in urban and stomach, bone and joint problems and tuberculosis in the district.

A majority of patients from minority community is found under the treatment of private allopathic physicians in rural, urban and in the district. Allopathic hospitals are commonly available followed by ayurvedic hospitals/dispensaries in rural (58.49 per cent), urban (45 per cent) and in the district (54.79 per cent) for medical treatment. Also, medical facility in rural areas for general ailment is found available at the block level, which is generally treated under PHC/CHC. Medical facilities for tuberculosis, eye ailments and other chronic diseases are generally available at the district head quarter, which are treated considerably under district hospital.

In urban areas, all minority households have reported that medical facilities for general ailments, MCH diseases, tuberculosis, eye-ailments and other chronic diseases are available within the area itself. Whereas, medical treatment of the general ailments and MCH diseases is carried out by the private physicians, the same for tuberculosis, eye ailments and other chronic diseases is performed under the government hospital.

In the district, the medical facilities for general ailments are available substantially within the area and that for MCH diseases at block level and the medical treatment of these diseases has been carried out substantially under

PHC/CHC. Medical facilities for tuberculosis, eye ailments and other chronic diseases are found available substantially at the district head quarters and medical treatment of these diseases has been carried out substantially under district hospital. However, a majority of minority households in rural (88.96 per cent), urban (83.91 per cent) and in the district (87.20 per cent) is found dissatisfied with the existing medical facilities. A majority of them in rural areas has demanded to open a dispensary at the village level; and those in urban areas and the district have demanded to prevent doctors from doing private practice.

Study also examines child mortality among minority community on account of various diseases, such as, (i) cholera, (ii) pneumonia, (iii) tetanus, (iv) jaundice, (v) diarrhoea, and (vi) whooping cough. A majority of male children in rural areas who died within 1 year, has suffered mainly from cholera and those who died during 1 to 5 years and upto 5 years of age are mainly due to diarrhoea The female child mortality upto 1 year has mainly been due to cholera and tetanus and those between 1 to 5 years and upto 5 years are due mainly to the cholera and tetanus. Thus, cholera, diarrhoea and tetanus are the major diseases for child mortality in rural areas.

In urban areas, the mortality of male child upto 5 years of age is found mainly due to cholera, jaundice, diarrhoea and whooping cough, while those of female mortality is caused mainly due to tetanus, diarrhoea and whooping cough. In the district, the main diseases of mortality among male children upto 5 years of age have been found to be cholera, tetanus and whooping cough, while those for female mortality are the diarrhoea, cholera, tetanus and whooping cough, in order of importance. The analysis, thus, underlines cholera, tetanus, diarrhoea and whooping cough as major diseases due to which child mortality has taken place.

Employment Structure, Welfare Programmes and Development of Minorities

Chapter V examines various aspects on employment, development programmes and the development of minorities. Finding suggests that a majority of minority population is engaged as self-employed in rural, while as skilled workers in urban and in the district. In the district, a majority of skilled workers and artisans is found dissatisfied, while to those of self-employed workers have expressed satisfaction. The principal reasons, in order of importance, for dissatisfaction of artisans are found to be the declining demand in the market, problem in marketing and irregular earning; for skilled workers, the exploitation by the middlemen followed by irregular earning; and for self-employed financial constraint and low profit margin. More than half of the minority households feel that their economic condition needs to be improved.

In rural areas, a majority of minority household members is found employed as agricultural labour (42.16 per cent) and non-agricultural labour (34.31 per cent). In urban areas, a majority of minority population is found employed in bidi making (28.21 per cent), in zari works (17.95 per cent) and in rickshaw pulling (10.27 per cent). Non-agricultural labour accounts for 7.69 per cent. The 5.13 per cent of minority population are found employed in each activity of kite making, TV/Radio repairing and compass making. In the district, a majority of minority population is found engaged as agricultural labour (30.49 per cent) and non-agricultural labour (26.95 per cent).

A majority of minority household members in rural areas has expressed their willingness to start new economic activity. The principal proposed economic activities in rural areas include : (i) general store, (ii) cloth selling, (iii) atta chakki, (iv) cycle repairing and parts, (v) pan shop and (vi) tea stall, which will involve finance per person of Rs.36,195.00, Rs.46,937.00, Rs.41,111.00, Rs.16,000.00,

Rs.12,875.00 and to Rs.11,000.00 respectively. In urban areas, the main proposed economic activities are: (i) general store, (ii) tea stall, (iii) motor binding, (iv) hotel, (v) cycle repairing and shop and (vi) electric shop, which will require finance per person of Rs.27,250.00, Rs.11,660.00, Rs.16,166.00, Rs.17,000.00, Rs.23,750.00 and to Rs.20,000.00 respectively. In the district, the principal proposed economic activities consist of: (i) general store, (ii) cloth selling, (iii) tea stall, (iv) cycle repairing and parts shop, (v) hotel and (vi) atta chakki, which will need finance per person of Rs.34,734.00, Rs.48,388.00, Rs.11,285.00, Rs.18,384.00, Rs.20,545.00 and to Rs.41,111.00 respectively. The financial requirement per person to start a proposed economic activity comes to Rs.32,755.00 in rural, Rs.22,026.00 in urban and to Rs.29,787.00 in the district, on an average.

In rural areas, the proposed economic activities are found generally advantageous in terms of employment generation, marketing and earnings. In urban areas, motor binding, cycle repairing and parts shop and electric shop are found advantageous in terms of marketing and earnings but these do not seem to have advantage in employment generation. Other proposed economic activities, like general store and tea stall and hotel are found advantageous in all respects. In the district, the principal proposed economic activities are found advantageous in all respects of employment generation, better marketing and high earning.

The analysis has further been extended to understand indepth the (i) training required for artisans and self-employed, (ii) finance and training required for un-employed youth and (iii) skills required for un-employed and self-employed youths. Findings suggest that, in rural areas, all artisans mainly require training in skills and in reducing the cost of production. Self-employed needs training in skill development and in reducing the cost of production. In urban areas, a majority of artisans requires training in skill development followed by reduction in the cost of production. A majority of self-employed requires training in entrepreneurship/ management and in marketing. In the district, whereas a majority of artisans requires training in skill development and reduction in the cost of production, the self-employed mainly needs training in entrepreneurship/ management. Un-employed youth in rural, urban and in the district needs financial support to improve their economic conditions. Across different economic activities, under-employed youths in rural, urban and in the district have required technical and educational skills mainly for efficiently doing the zari work. Self-employed and under-employed youths in rural, urban and in the district have demanded financial support as critical requirement for improving their economic efficiency and thereby their economic conditions.

Study further examines the impact of development programmes initiated by the government from time to time. Findings suggest that development programmes, such as, Total Literacy Campaign, Computer Education and Non-Formal Education are beneficial for the minority household members in rural areas, while Literacy Campaign and Coaching facility are found beneficial in urban areas. Between rural and urban, development programmes are found more beneficial in the former than that in the later. Also, financial requirement in terms of loans and subsidies have been extended by DRDA and banks to members of the minority households in rural areas to create employment and self-employment mainly from artisanal/handi-craft/ handloom/house-hold activities through Gram Sabha. In urban areas, loans and subsidies given by the banks have mainly generated employment from artisanal/handicraft/ hand-loom/household and in trade and business activities.

The employment generated has been found to be about 43 days per person in rural areas, being highest 150 days each from self-employment in trade/ business and seasonal activities, while lowest of 33 days from employment generating programmes and schemes. In urban areas, employment generated has been found to be 180 days per person, being highest 270 days per person from self-employment in trade/business, while lowest of 60 days from employment generating programmes/schemes. In the district, employment generated comes to about 87 days per person, being highest 210 days per person from self-employment in trade/business, while lowest about 35 days per person from employment generating programmes and schemes.

In rural areas, income comes to Rs.2,454.00 per person, highest being Rs.9,445.00 per person from self-employment in trade/business, while lowest of Rs.1,707.00 per person from employment generating programmes and schemes. In urban areas, income comes to Rs.9,063.00 per person, being highest of Rs.10,000.00 each from self-employment in trade/business and self-employment in artisonal/ handicraft/houschold activity, while lowest of Rs.3,714.00 per person from employment generating schemes and programmes. In the district, income generated has been found to be Rs.4,543.00 per person, being highest to Rs.9,723.00 per person from self-employment in trade/ business, while lowest to Rs.1,828.00 per person from employment generating schemes and programmes. General finding, thus, suggests that self-employment in trade/ business is higher from employment and income generating activity, whereas, employment generating programmes and schemes pursued by the government emerges as the least employment and income generating in rural, urban and in the district. It may be mentioned that a majority of minority households in rural (89.88 per cent), urban (70.14 per cent) and in the district (83 per cent) is found unaware about the coaching facilities available for competitive examinations.

A majority of households in rural areas is of the opinion that reservation of minorities in government jobs at the district level, representation of minorities in development works at village level, free education facilities and development of cottage industries at the village level would be pre-requisite for the development of minorities. In urban areas, a majority of households feels that effective utilization of welfare schemes and development of cottage industries at the city level and reservation of minorities in all government services at the district level would be essential for the development of minority community. In the district, a majority of households feels the reservation of minorities in all government services at the district level, awareness about the government schemes at the village level and its effective utilization at the city level are required to be undertaken for the development of minorities.

We have also examined the role of factors affecting the growth of entrepreneurship of minorities employed in manufacturing, artisanal and in self-employed activities. In urban and in the district, entrepreneurship in manufacturing has mainly been affected on account of (i) shortage of finance, (ii) severe competition with large units/ entrepreneurs, (iii) lack of awareness about development programmes, etc., in order of importance. In rural artisonal activities, entrepreneurship has mainly been affected by the (i) lack of initiative, (ii) lack of knowledge, (iii) limited scope/market for the product, (iv) lack of managerial skills, (v) lack of training facility in skill development, (vi) absence of institutional support for marketing of products/ services, etc. Artisonal activities in urban areas are affected due to such factors as (i) shortage of finance, (ii) absence of institution/organization to protect wages/exploitation of artisans, etc.; and, in the district these include : (i) inadequate institutional support for marketing of products/services, (ii) absence of institution/organization to protect wages/ exploitation of artisans, (iii) shortage of finance, etc. In self-employed activities, entrepreneurship in rural, urban and in the district has been found affected due mainly to

(i) shortage of finance, (ii) lack of awareness about development programmes, etc.

Finding, thus, suggests that growth of entrepreneurship has generally been affected by the (i) inadequate financial support, (ii) lack of awareness about the development programmes, (iii) severe competition with large units/ entrepreneurs. Study also reveals that common community assets, such as, worship place is used exclusively for worshipping, open field for playing, madarsa exclusively for studying in rural and urban areas. Library and park in urban areas are found used for studying and play ground respectively.

We have also inquired from minority households about the measures for their socio-economic development. A majority of minority households in rural and urban feels that free education with scholarship may enhance their educational development. In the district, besides above, technical and employment generating education and girl's education have also been emphasized. Subsequently, financial support and development of cottage industries have been given due consideration for economic development in rural, urban and in the district. For health improvement, opening up of PHC in villages and free medicine facility in rural; and free medicine facility and awareness about family planning programmes in urban and in the district have mainly been realized. Apart from these, housing along with roads and drainage facility to weaker sections have mainly been underlined for housing and sanitary development in rural, urban and in the district. Also, effective utilization of welfare schemes of the government through publicity and planning at the grass root level, while productive use of man power resources through technical training have been recognized by the majority of minority households in rural, urban and in the district.

Recommendations for Policy Action

Findings of the study are not without policy relevance. Various recommendations have emerged, which, Department of Minorities Welfare and Muslim Waqfs, Government of Uttar Pradesh, may adopt for the development of minorities. In view of analytical convenience, recommendations though overlapping in character arising out of the general findings of the study have been discussed as here under :

A. Social Development of Minorities

1. As over half of the minority population has been found illiterates, it would be useful to implement Total Literacy Campaign effectively so that all minority households are covered under this programme in the district.

2. As a majority of minority children is found educated upto primary level and that these have received education mainly in government schools, private schools and madarsas, it is necessary that awareness campaign about the importance of education after Vth Standard is undertaken. This could be even done by organizing the seminars, conferences either by government organizations or by NGOs. It may also be done by providing the incentives in terms of free education with scholarship, free reading materials, stationery and mèal to the minority students, willing to study after Vth standard.

It is recommended that scholarship amounting to Rs.50 per month per minority student needs to be provided for continuing their education after Vth Standard. Also, the government schools, private schools and madarsas are required to be increased along with the Urdu teachers at block and possibly at the village level so that paucity of suitable educational institutions may not be a problem for continuing education after primary level. Besides, it would also be useful if professional education is linked with traditional teaching beyond Vth standard of education. It would help minority students to earn livelihood along with studies simultaneously. Care, however, needs to be taken to avoid the misuse of incentives.

3. As enrolment of minorities has declined from lower age profile to higher age profile and that poor economic condition of parents is found significant contributory factor for this, it is essential that income level of the household is enhanced. This could be done by establishing cottage industries extensively at the village and at the block level. First step, therefore, would be to establish the cottage industries and to extend sufficient skills and financial assistance at least for 5 years. This would lead the educational development for minority children. It may, however, be stressed that such measures of the government through Minority Finance and Development Corporation and District Minority Welfare Department need to be followed as a temporary device for educational development, which may be discontinued after minority households become economically self-sufficient.

B. Economic Development

4. Findings suggest that a majority of members of minority household in rural areas is employed as self-employed personnel and artisans. Whereas the self-employed have faced the problems of low demand, poor marketing and irregular earnings, the self-employed personnel have faced the problems in terms of finance and low profit. To the extent, artisans have faced the problem due to inefficient marketing and low profit margins, it would be useful to establish Marketing Cooperative Societies for efficient marketing for the products produced by minority artisans. The minority artisans would be automatically the members of such society. It would help in marketing of their products and earning the profits.

To the extent self-employed has faced the financial constraint, with low profit margin, it would be necessary to make financial resources available to them. It is recommended that a special arrangement is required to be made to extend loan facility either from commercial and non-commercial banks at the affordable rate of interest or from Minority Finance and Development Corporation (MFDC). MFDC is specifically established to extend financial assistance only to the minorities, which, to a very large extent, is not popular among the minorities. Thus, it is recommended that banks as well as MFDC will have to make special provision to meet the financial requirement for the self-employed personnel among minority community.

5. It may be recapitulated that in rural areas, a majority of minority household members has expressed willingness to start new economic activities, such as, (i) general store, (ii) cloth selling, (iii) atta chakki, (iv) cycle repairing and parts, (v) pan shop, (vi) tea stall, etc. In urban areas, these include : (i) general store, (ii) tea stall, (iii) motor binding, (iv) hotel, (v) cycle repairing and parts shop, (vi) electric shop, etc.; and in the district, such activities are : (i) general store, (ii) cloth selling, (iii) tea stall, (iv) cycle repairing and parts shop, (v) hotel and (vi) atta chakki. Most of the proposed economic activities are found advantageous in terms of employment and income generation and marketing.

Thus, from the view point of development of minorities, such activities are required to be encouraged. Also, efforts are required to overcome the problems faced in starting principal proposed economic activities. In view of this, it is recommended that finance required to start such economic activities, say upto Rs.50,000 per person be financed for 5 years either by the commercial or non-commercial banks at affordable rate of interest. Minority Finance and Development Corporation may extend loan facility at the rate of 4 per cent per annum, instead of 6 per cent currently existing therein, along with 25 per cent of subsidies on the loans. Also, margin money of 10 per cent payable by the entrepreneurs needs to be removed. In doing so, however, care needs to be taken to enhance the full utilization of loans rather than making gains from the soft loans, subsidies and margin money.

6. It may be advisable that above identified economically gainful activities need to be given special consideration within existing rural development programmes. May be that District Minority Development Department is entrusted to advise block officials to encourage minority households to start identified economically gainful activities within the existing rural development programmes/schemes.

7. Findings suggest that artisans and self-employed personnel in rural, urban and in the district have generally required training in skill development, reducing the cost of production, training in entrepreneurship/management and in marketing. It would be desirable that artisans and self-employed are sent to the similar type of units for skill development, acquiring expertise for reducing the cost of production and training for efficient marketing. Alternatively, it may also be done by inviting persons from similar type of units, which are fully aware about skill development, cost reducing measures and marketing. After, training is completed, trainers may be sent back to their parental unit/establishment.

As far training in entrepreneurship is concerned, artisans and self-employed personnel may even join the various training programmes organised from time to time by Entrepreneurship Development Institute or by similar type of organizations. May be that the Department of Minorities Welfare and Muslim Waqfs with the help of research organizations or reliable NGOs may also start training courses so as to improve and enhance the entrepreneurship/ management for artisans and self-employed and under-employed among the minorities.

8. Finding further reveals that self-employment in trade/ business is highly employment and income generating

activities, while employment generating programmes/ schemes pursued by the government is found to be of least importance. Trade and business has generated annually the employment of 150 days per person in rural, 180 days per person in urban and to 210 days in the district. The income generated per person comes to Rs.9,445 in rural, Rs.10,000 in urban and to Rs.9,723 in the district. Thus, trade and business activity needs to be encouraged. Such activities including general store as discussed earlier are required to be enhanced. It is recommended that a special training programme for educating various aspects of trade/ business may also yield a desirable results.

9. Findings suggest that growth of entrepreneurship for artisans, self-employed and those engaged in non-rural manufacturing has mainly been affected by (a) inadequate financial support, (b) lack of awareness about development programmes, (c) severe competition with large units/ entrepreneurs, etc.

Various problems under the way of development of entrepreneurship, therefore, need to be overcome on a priority basis. In doing so, it would be useful for minorities to understand deeply about marketing potential product by product; to develop product-wise managerial skills; to have a sufficient knowledge about the financial assistance available from different financial institutions; and awareness about the development programmes and have the capacity to extract benefit from these programmes. All these structural problems may not be solved only through the efforts by the government alone. In fact, a cooperative move is required through a formal structured organizations, such as, Department of District Minority Welfare with the active participation by the minorities engaged as self-employed, artisans and those engaged in manufacturing.

What is essentially required is the organization of training programmes for minorities frequently and in such programmes, courses on marketing, different channels of finance, competition faced from rivals in production and marketing, profit potential and the level of exploitation by the middlemen are required to be taught by the experts on the concerned disciplines. It is recommended that finance for such training courses be provided by the Department of Minorities Welfare and Muslim Waqfs to the District Minority Welfare Department.

10. As 33.13 per cent of minority households in rural, 34.18 per cent in urban and to 33.60 per cent in the urban are found living below the poverty line, an immediate action is required towards this direction. It would be advisable if special consideration is given for the minority households living below the poverty line. May be that reservation for minority households is made within the existing rural development programmes according to their representation in the total district population. It may also be possible if block level officials are instructed to give special weightage to minority households by the District Minority Welfare Department. Thus, positive contribution by block and District Minority Welfare Department can help in bringing up the minority households above the poverty line.

C. Housing and Health Improvement

11. General findings suggest that a majority of houses is kutcha in rural areas, while pucca in urban and semi-kutcha in the district. Thus, entire housing structure needs to be revamped. To do this requires a special provision for financial assistance by the Minority Finance and Development Corporation particularly for the rural minority households. The amount of housing loan may be determined by examining the repayable capacity of the minority households and the feasibility of requirement. The repayment period is also required to be extended say for 25 years. Rate of interest is also required to be brought down, say at

3 per cent per annum. Also, margin money of 15 per cent seems to be unnecessary, which needs to be reduced to 5 per cent. This would help in converting kutcha houses into pucca houses. On government side, electrification is also called for in the minority dominated villages in the district.

12. Finding further suggests that a majority of minority population has suffered from respiratory disorder, stomach problem, bone and joint and tuberculosis in rural, stomach, tuberculosis and heart problem in urban and that of stomach, bone and joint and tuberculosis in the district. These are generally treated by private allopathic physicians. Medical facilities for different diseases available at village level, block level and at the district level are not sufficient. It is, therefore, recommended that at least one dispensary be opened in each village and that doctors employed in government hospitals, must be prevented from doing the private practices.

13. Also, cholera, tetanus, diarrhoea and whooping cough are found to be the main cause for child mortality. It is, therefore, recommended that expert doctors for the treatment of these diseases must be made available in private allopathic hospitals, PHC/CHC, government hospitals, ayurvedic hospitals and homeopathic hospitals. It is recommended that doctors having expertise about these diseases are appointed on priority basis. Such policy recommendations are required to be followed immediately.

14. Present study following the 'area based' approach does not, however, provide separate plan for development of minorities based on cost and benefit, but it provides certain specific policy guidelines within the existing rural development programmes. It would be useful if Department of Minorities Welfare and Muslim Waqfs, Government of Uttar Pradesh may advise and monitor the District Minority Welfare Department in implementing above policy guidelines, which, in turn, may advise the block officials

to expedite the policy measures in proper perspective. This would lead to socio-economic development of minorities within the prevailing socio-economic rural development programmes.

It may, however, be noted that various policy measures recommended need to be treated as temporary device for development of minorities. If these are treated as permanent 'stretches' it is recommended that these must immediately be withdrawn. Also, policy incentives must be used for the purpose for which it is extended and that its misuse must be avoided. These are some of the policy recommendations derived from the 'area based' and 'population end approach' rather than 'programme end approach' emerging out of the general findings of the present study consistent with socioeconomic development of minorities in the Rampur district.

Bibliography

Aiyar, Swaminathan, S. Anklesaria, "Encouraging News About Poverty", *The Economic Times*, December 14, 1995, p. 7.

Alagh, Yoginder, K., "Poverty and Food Security Towards a Policy System for Food Security", *Economic and Political Weekly,* Vol. XXX, No. 52, December 30, 1995, pp. A.142-150.

Alawode, Abayomia, "Some Reflections on the Role of Stock Market in Economic Development", *The Indian Journal of Economics*, Vol. LXVII, No. 305, October, 1996, pp. 249-260.

Bajpai, Nirupum, "Economic Reforms in Developing Countries: Theory and Evidence", *Economic and Political Weekly*, Vol. XXX, No. 1, January 7, 1995, pp. 113-118.

Baker, Lawrence, C. and Cots, Kenneth, S., "HMO penetration and the cost of health care: Market discipline or market segmentation", *The American Economic Review*, Vol. 86, No. 2, May 1996, pp. 389-394.

Bal, Arul, "Protecting Health Care Consumers: Is CPA Effective?", *Economic and Political Weekly*, Vol. XXXI, No. 51, December 21, 1996, pp. 3289-3290.

Balakrishnan, Rajiv, "India on the Eve of Copenhagen Summit: Issues in the Social Development", *Economic and Political Weekly*, Vol. XXX, No. 11, March 18, 1995, pp. 548-553.

Balakrishna, S., "Poverty Correlates and Surrogates",

Journal of Rural Development, Vo. 14, No. 3, July-September, 1995, pp. 261-286.

Balakrishna, S., "A Guide to Social Analysis for Projects in Developing Countries (Book Reviews)", *Journal of Rural Development*, Vol. 14, No .4,- October-December, 1995, pp. 457-458.

Banik, Arindam, "Poverty in Bangladesh", *Economic and Political Weekly*, Vol. XXXI, Nos.2 & 3, January 13-20, 1996, p. 94.

Bardhan, P., "Efficiency, Equity and Poverty Alleviation: Policy Issues in Less Developed Countries", *The Economic Journal*, Vol. 106, No. 438, September 1996, pp 1344-1355.

Begam, Hajira, Sahoo, Satya, Sanda and Mohsin, Mohd., "Work Participation and Labour Supply of Muslim Women: Determinants Models", *Indian Journal of Economics*, Vol. LXXX, Part III, No. 298, 1995, pp. 363-396.

Benabou, Ronald, "Heterogeneity, Stratification and Growth Macro-Economic Implications of Community Structure and School Finance", *The American Economic Review*, Vol. 86, No. 3, June, 1996, pp. 584-603.

Bhat, Sham K., "Export and Economic Growth in India", *Artha Vijnana*, Vol. XXXVI, No. 4, December 1995, pp. 350-358.

Bhoosnurmath, Kashinath, "District Development Policy Statement", *Journal of Rural Development*, Vol. 13, No. 2, April-June, 1994, pp. 287-294.

Boadway, Robin Marceau, Nicolas and Marchand Mauric, "Investment in Education and the Time Inconsistency of Redistributive Tax Policy", *Economica*, Vol. 63, No. 250, May 1996, pp. 171-189.

Bolding, Alex, Mollings, Peter, P. and Straaten, Kess, Van. "Modules for Modernization: Colonial Irrigation in India and the Technological Dimension of Agrarian Change", *Journal of Development Studies*, Vol. 31, No. 6, August 1995, pp. 805-844.

Carrington, William, J., Detragiache, Enrica and Vishwanath, Tara, "Migration with Endogenous Moving Costs", *American-Economic Review*, Vol. 86, No. 4, September, 1996, pp. 909-928.

Chadha, G.K., "Employment, Earnings and Poverty: A Study of Rural India and Indonesia", *Anuvesak*, Vol. 25, No. 1, January-June, 1995, pp. 135-137.

Chalkley, M. and Malcomson, J.M., "Policy Forum: Health Resources and Health Care", *The Economic Journal*, Vol. 106, No. 439, November, 1996, pp. 1689-1691.

Chenoy, Anuradha, M., "Islam and Identity in Contemporary Central Asia", *Economic and Political Weekly*, Vol. XXXI, No. 9, March 2, 1996, p. 518.

Chhata, Ashwini, "A Socio-Ecological Basis for Natural Resource Management: Forest Bill Debate", *Economic and Political Weekly*, Vol. XXXI, No. 18, May 4, 1996, pp. 1084-1090.

Clarc, Andres Rodriguez, "Multinationals, Linkages and Economic Development", *The American Economic Review*, Vol. 86, No. 4, September 1996, pp. 852-873.

Currie, Janet and Gruber Jonathan, "Health Insurance Eligibility, Utilization of Medical Care and Child Health", *Quarterly Journal of Economics*, Vol. CXI, Issue 2, May 1996, pp. 431-464.

Cutler, David M. and Gruber, Jonathan, "The Effect of Medicaid Expansions on Public Insurance, Private Insurance and Redistribution", *The American Economic Review*, Vol. 86, No. 2, May 1996, pp. 378-383.

Dasgupta, Biplab, "The New Political Economy: A Critical

Analysis", *Economic and Political Weekly*, Vol. XXXII, No. 4, January 25, 1997, p. PE-13.

Datta, Pranati, "Inter-State Migration in India", *Indian Journal of Regional Science*, Vol. XXVIII, No. 2, 1996, pp. 55-68.

Debi, Sailabala, "Regional Inequalities in Education in Orissa", *Indian Journal of Regional Science*, Vol. XXVIII, No. 2, 1996, pp. 11-24.

Deoghare, P.R., Rekib, A., Sood, S.B., "Goat Rearing: Prospects and Importance", *Yojana*, Vol. 40, No. 3, March 1996, pp. 29-30.

Department of Economics and Statistics, *Statistical Bulletin*, District Rampur, 1994, State Planning Institute, U.P.

Desai, Bhupat M., "Growth with Social Justice", *Economic and Political Weekly*, Vol. XXX, No. 47, November 1995, pp. 3019-3020.

Diwan, Romesh, "Is there hope for the Indian Economy?", *Economic and Political Weekly*, Vol. XXX, No. 10, March 11, 1995, pp. 527-528.

Duggal, Ravi, Nandraj, Sunil, Vadair Asha, "Health Expenditure Across States", Part-I, *Economic and Political Weekly*, Vol. XXX, No. 15, April 15, 1995, pp. 834-838.

Durga, P., Kahaka and Murty, K.N., "Projection Using Flexible Demand System for India", *Arth Vijnana*, Vol. XXXVII, No. 2, June 1995, pp. 138-155.

Dutta, Bijit Kumar, "A Model for Rural Development: The Entrepreneurial Diffusion Approach", *Indian Journal of Economics*, Vol. LXXVI, Part-I, No. 300, 1995, pp. 23-30.

Dutta, Surjit K. and Ghosh, Dilip, K., "Poverty Alleviation and Decentralized Rural Development in India: A Case Study in West Bengal", *Anuveshak*, Vol. 25, No. 1, January-June, 1995, pp. 73-87.

Erappa (Dr.), S., "Determinants of Development: An Analysis", *Yojana*, Vol. 40, No. 7, July 1996, pp. 12-13.

Engineer, Asgar Ali, "Understanding Islam", *Economic and Political Weekly*, Vol. XXXI, January 13-20, 1996, p. 93.

Fernandez, Raquel and Rogerson Richard, "Income Distribution, Communities and the Quality of Public Education", *Quarterly Journal of Economics*, Vol. CXI, Issue 1, February 1996, pp. 135-164.

Fuchs, Victor, R., "Economics Values and Health Care Reform", *The American Economic Review*, Vol. 86, No. 1, March 1996, pp. 1-24.

Galor, Oded and Weil, David, N., "The Gender Gap, Fertility and Growth", *The American Economic Review*, Vol. 86, No. 3, June 1996, pp. 374-387.

Gazetteer of India, District Rampur, Government of Uttar Pradesh, Department of District Gazetteer, U.P., 1974.

Ghosh, Arun, "Health Care and Globalisation: Case for Selective Approach," *Economic and Political Weekly*, Vol. XXXI, No. 8, February 24, 1996, pp. 441-442.

Ghosh, Arun, "Poverty Surplus Labour and Development Strategies",. *Economic and Political Weekly*, Vol. XXXII, No. 8, February 22, 1997, pp. 403-405.

Gill, Sucha Singh, "Punjab: Privatising Health Care", *Economic and Political Weekly*, Vol. XXXI, No. 1, January 6, 1996, pp. 18-19.

Gill, Sucha Singh, Brar and Jaswinder Singh, "Global Market and Competitiveness of Indian Agriculture: Some Issues", *Economic and Political Weekly,* Vol. XXXI, No. 32, August 10, 1996, pp. 2167-2177.

Goel, Sangeeta, "Economic Perspective's on Displacement", *Economic and Political Weekly*, Vol. XXXI, No. 24, June 15, 1996, pp. 1461-1467.

Greenaway, David, "Policy Forum, Health Care Reform", *The Economic Journal*, Vol. 106, No. 439, November 1996, p. 1689.

Groolaert, Christian and Kanbur Ravi, "The Lucky Few Amidst Economic Decline: Distributional Change in Cote dloire as seen through Panel Data Sets 1985-88", *Journal of Development Studies*, Vol. 31, No. 4, April 1995, pp. 603-619.

Grossman, Gene, M. and Krueger, Alen, B., "Economic Growth and the Environment", *The Quarterly Journal of Economics*, Vol. CX, Issue 2, May 1996, pp. 321-352.

Gulati, S.C., "District Level Development Indices: A Factor Analytical Approach", *Indian Journal of Regional Science*, Vol. XXVIII, No. 1, 1996, pp. 97-106.

Gupta, Arjun, Sen, "Financial Sector and Economic Reforms in India", *Economic and Political Weekly,* Vol. XXX, No. 1, January 7, 1995, pp. 276-284.

Hanratty, Maria J., "Canadian National Health Insurance and Infant Health", *The American Economic Review*, Vol. 86, No. 1, March, 1996, pp. 276-284.

Hanumappa, H.G., "Rural Development and Indicators of Rural Welfare", *Yojana*, Vol. 40, No. 3, March 1996, pp. 9-11 and 15.

Hasan, Mushirul, "Muslim Intellectuals, Institutions and the Post-Colonial Predicament", *Economic and Political Weekly*, Vol. XXX, No. 47, November 25, 1995, pp. 22-75.

Hashim, S.R., "Dimensions of Poverty and Approach to Poverty Alleviation", *Yojana*, Vol. 40, No. 11, November 1996, pp. 5-11.

Heller, Patrick, "From Class Struggles to Class Compromise: Redistribution and Growth in South Indian States", *Journal of Development Studies*, Vol. 31, No. 5, June 1995, pp. 645-672.

Jafri, S.S.A., "Sunni Auqaf and Waqf Board of Uttar Pradesh in a Shample: A Critical Analysis", in a book: *Waqf Administration: Status and Issues,* Edited by Prof. S.K. Singh, Spell Bound Publications,1998. Also published in *Economic and Political Weekly*, Vol. XXXII, No. 25, June 21-27, 199y.

Jafri, S.S.A., "Socio-Economic Development of Muslims in Urban Settlements of Avadh Region, Uttar Pradesh: A Comparative Analysis", in a book: *Muslims in India* by Prof. (Emeritus) S.N. Singh, Anmol Publications Pvt. Ltd., New Delhi, 2003.

Jafri, S.S.A., "Socio-Economic Conditions of Downtrodden Minorities (Muslims) in Lucknow Metropolis", GIDS Project, 2004.

Jafri, S.S.A. and Abhilasha Srivastava, "Spatial Pattern and Concentration of Muslim Household Workers in Uttar Pradesh: A Comparative Analysis", in *National Seminar on Muslim Artisan, Craftsman and Traders in India*, held at AMU Aligarh, February 2005.

Jafri, S.S.A. and Abhilasha Srivastava, "Muslim Household Workers in Urban Areas of Uttar Pradesh: A Comparative Analysis", in *National Seminar on India's Developemnt Concerns*, held at Lucknow University, March 2005.

Jafri, S.S.A., "Population and Education Dynamics Among Backward and Forward Castes of Downtrodden Muslims in Lucknow Metropolis", in *Social Science Journal of Islam and Muslim Societies*, Serial Publications, New Delhi, 2005.

Jethanandani, Kishore, "Rethinking Poverty Alleviation", *The Economic Times*, February 17, 1996, p. 5.

Jha, D., "An Outlook for Rural Development of India", *Journal of Rural Development*, Vol. 13, No. 1, January-March 1994, pp. 129-132.

Jhunjhunwala, Bharat, "UNICEF and Poverty: Trat not Merely the Symptoms", *The Economic Times*, February 28, 1996, p. 6.

John, O. Ommen, "Role of Panchayati Raj in Educational Administration", *Journal of Rural Development*, Vol. 13, No. 2, April-June, 1994, pp. 181-188.

Jose, P.D., "Participative Management of Development Programmes", *Journal of Rural Development*, Vol. 13, No. 4, October-December, 1994, pp. 515-526.

Kabra, Kamal Nayan, "Indian Planning and Liberalization", *Economic and Political Weekly*, Vol. XXXI, No. 40, October 5, 1996, pp. 2740-2745.

Kalegaonkar, Archana, "Pursuing Third World Women's Interests: Compatibility of Feminism with Grass Roots Development", *Economic and Political Weekly*, Vol. XXXII, No. 17, April 26-May 2, 1997, pp. WS.2-4 (Review of Women Studies).

Karkal, Malini, "What Does the National Family Health Survey Reveal", *Economic and Political Weekly*, Vol. XXXI, No. 15, April 13, 1996, pp. 931-934.

Kausal, Neeraj, "Abolishing Poverty Statistically", *The Economic Times*, January 1, 1996, p. 4.

Kessler, Daniel and Mcchellan, Mark, "Do Doctors Practice Defensive Medicines?", *Quarterly Journal of Economics*, Vol. CXI, No. 2, May 1996, pp. 353-390.

Khan, J.S., Brat Chetna and Seth, N.D., "Cultivation and Processing of Aromatic Plants for Rural Development", *Journal of Rural Development*, Vol. 13, No. 1, January-March, 1994, pp. 57-52.

Kishindo, Paul, "Land Reform and Agricultural Development: The Case of Levotho", *Journal of Rural Development*, Vol. 13, No .3, July-September, 1994, pp. 319-326.

Kohli, Anju and Kothari, Sadhna, "Occupational Structure of Population in Rajasthan: A Spatial Analysis

(1991)", *Indian Journal of Regional Science*, Vol. XXVIII, No. 2, 1996, pp. 25-32.

Kojima, R., "Introduction: Population Migration and Urbanization in Developing Countries", *Developing Economics*, Vol. XXXIV, No. 4, December 1996, pp. 349-369.

Kothari, Krishna, "Economic Impact of Rural Development Projects on Small Farmers", *Journal of Rural Development*, Vol. 13, No. 2, April-June 1994, pp. 199-226.

Krishnaji, N., "Working Mother and Child Survival in Rural India: Insights from Spatial Pattern", *Economic and Political Weekly*, Vol. XXX, No. 44, November 1995, pp. 2803-2808.

Krishnamurthy, K, Pandit, V., Palanivel, T., Saibaba, P. and Pratap, D., "Indian Economy, 1995-96 to 1997-98: An Alternative Scenarios", *Economic and Political Weekly*, Vol. XXXI, No. 11, March 16, 1996, pp. 661-672.

Kumar, Arun, "New Economic Policies, Instability and Policy Ineffectiveness", *Economic and Political Weekly*, Vol. XXXI, No. 47, November 23, 1996, pp. 3061-3070.

Kumar, Prahlad, "Restructuring Educational Programme in the Changing Liberalized Environment: Some Prescriptions for Growing Economic Like Malaysia", *The Indian Journal of Economics*, Vol. LXXVI, No. 303, April 1996, pp. 511-526.

Kumar, T. Krishna, "Management of Development in the Newly Emerging Global Economic Environment", *Economic and Political Weekly*, Vol. XXXI, No. 25, June 22, 1996, pp. 1578-1600.

Kundu, Amitabh and Gupta, Shalini, "Migration, Urbanization and Regional Inequality", *Economic and Political Weekly*, Vol. XXXI, No. 52, December 28, 1996, pp. 3391-3398.

Lanjouw, P. and Ravallion, M., "Poverty and Household Size", *The Economic Journal*, Vol. 103, No. 433, November, 1995, pp. 1415-1435.

Lerman, Robert, I., "The Impact of the Changing Vs. Family Structure on Child Poverty and Income Inequality", *Economics*, Vol. 63, No. 250(S), September, 1996, pp. 5119-5140.

Lowre, John, M. and Sen Ashish, "Gravity Model Applications in Health Planning", *Journal of Regional Sciences*, Vol. 36, No. 3, 1996, pp. 437-461.

Madhok, Alka, "Child Labour: Some Issues, Some Suggestions", *Yojana*, Vol. 40, No. 5, May 1996, pp. 27-29.

Malho, Ian, "Migrant Inertia, Accessibility and Local Unemployment", *Economics*, Vol. 62, No. 245, February 1995, pp. 123-132.

Mallick, Sushanta Kumar, "Causality Between Exports and Economic Growth in India: Evidence from Cointegration Based Error Correction Models", *The Indian Journal of Economics*, Vol. LXXVI, No. 302, January 1996, pp. 307-320.

Martina, Ala, "Ranking Poverty Levels in India: Some Theoretical Considerations", *Indian Economic Journal*, Vol. 43, No. 4, April-June, 1995-96, pp. 13-29.

Mathew, E.T., "Educated Unemployment in Kerala: Some Socio-Economic Aspect", *Economic and Political Weekly*, Vol. XXX, No. 6, February 1995, pp. 325-335.

Mathur, Kuldeep, "Politics and Implementation of Integrated Rural Development Programmes", *Economic and Political Weekly*, Vol. XXX, Nos. 41&42, October 14-21, 1995, pp. 2703-2708.

Meher, Rajkishor, "The Handloom Industry and the Socio-Economic Conditions of Weavers in Orissa", *Journal of Rural Development*, Vol. 14, No. 3, July-September, 1995, pp. 301-321.

Mishra, Chaturanan, "Role of Rural Labour in Socio-Economic and Political Transformation of India", *Indian Journal of Labour Economics*, Vol. 36, No. 1, January-March, 1993, pp. 77-79.

Mishra, V.N., Hazell, Peter, B.R., "Terms of Trade, Rural Poverty, Technology and Investment: The Indian Experience: 1952-53 to 1990-91", *Economic and Political Weekly*, Vol. XXXI, No. 13, March 30, 1996, pp. A-2-A-14.

Misry, Malika, "Will Muslims Outnumber Hindus", *The Economic Times*, November 25, 1995, p. 7.

Mitra, Arup, "Rural Non-Farm Employment, Poverty and Women", *Indian Journal of Labour Economics*, Vol. 36, No. 3, July-September, 1993, pp. 455-469.

Mohsin, M., Sridhvi, S. and Kamaiah, B., "Wagner's Law in Developing Countries: Evidence from Time Series Analysis", *Artha Vijnana*, Vol. XXXVII, No. 3, September 1995, pp. 231-250.

Mollick, Sushanta Kumar and Kumar, T. Krishna, "A Non-Econometric Review of Indian Macro-Economic Models", *Artha Vijnana*, Vol. XXXVII, No. 1, March 1995, pp. 1-45.

Morrissery, Oliver and Rai, Yogesh, "The GATT Agreement on Trade Related Investment Measures: Implications for Developing Countries and their Relationship with Transitional Corporation", *Journal of Developing Studies*, Vol. 31, No. 5, June 1995, pp. 702-724.

Murthy, Venkatesha, G.B., "Minority Status and Fertility", *Economic and Political Weekly*, Vol. XXXI, No. 20, May 18, 1996, p. 1224.

Muthayya, B.C., "Challenges Facing Agriculture and Rural Development", *Journal of Rural Development*, Vol. 13, No. 4, October-December, 1994, pp. 603-604.

Nair, K.R.G, "Reservation Policy for Small Industry", *Economic and Political Weekly*, Vol. XXX, No. 35, September 2, 1995, pp. 2210-2211.

Nellithanam, Rahul, Jacob, "Green Revolution and Subsistence Agriculture: You Reap as You Sow", *Economic and Political Weekly*, Vol. XXXII, No. 18, May 3-9, 1997, pp. 930-932.

Ogawa, Naobiro and Ermisch, John, F., "Family Structure, Home Time Demands and the Employment Patterns of Japanese Married Women", *Journal of Labour Economics*, Vol. 14, No. 4, October 1996, pp. 677-702.

Otsuka, Kejjiro, Gasscon Fe. and Asano, Seki, "Green Revolution and Labour demand in Rice Farming: The Case of Central Lazon, 1966-90", *The Journal of Development Studies*, Vol. 31, No. 1, October, 1994, pp. 82-110.

Pal, Krishna Gopal, "Regional Disparities in Economic Development: An Inter-District Empirical Study of the State of West Bengal", *Artha Vijnana*, Vol. XXXVII, No. 3, September 1995, pp. 276-296.

Palibandla, Murali, "Firm Size and Export Behaviour: An Indian Case Study", *Journal of Development Studies*, Vol. 31, No. 6, August 1995, pp. 868-882.

Panikkar, K.N., "Culture and Globalisation: A Non-Issue at World Summit on Social Development", *Economic and Political Weekly*, Vol. XXX, Nos.7&8, February 18-25, 1995, pp. 374-375.

Papola, T.S., "Employment Growth and Social Protection of Labour in India", *Indian Journal of Industrial Relations*, ol.30, No. 2, October 1994, pp. 117-143.

Park, Ki Seong, "Economic Growth and Multi-Skilled Workers in Manufacturing", *Journal of Labour Economics*, Vol. 14, No. 2, April 1996, pp. 254-285.

Parsuramam, S., "Relief Assistance and Rehabilitation

Lessons in Disaster Management", *Economic and Political Weekly*, Vol. XXX, No. 27, July 8, 1995, p. 1654.

Patnaik, Prabhat and Chandrasekhar, C.P., "Indian Economy under Structural Adjustment", *Economic and Political Weekly*, Vol. XXX, No. 47, November 25, 1995, pp. 3001-3013.

Pattanaik, "Gender Justice, Women Empowerment and Maternal Health", *Yojana*, Vol. 40, No. 11, November 1996, pp. 31-33.

Prasad, C., Hemlatha, "Development of Women and Child in Rural Areas: Successful Case Studies," *Journal of Rural Development*, Vol. 14, No. 1, January-March 1995, pp. 65-88.

Purohit, Brijesh, C., "Health Budget of Rajasthan", *The Economic Times*, August 30, 1995, p. 7.

Purushottam, P., "Marketing of Non-Farm Rural Products", *Journal of Rural Development*, Vol. 13, No. 3, July-September 1994, p. 472.

Raju, K.A., "Rural Development in India: A Public Policy Approach", *Journal of Rural Development*, Vol. 14, No. 1, January-March, 1995, p. 89.

Ramachandran, V.K., Rawal, Vikas and Swaminathan, Madhura, "Investments Gaps in Primary Education: A State-wise Study", *Economic and Political Weekly*, Vol. XXXII, Nos.1&2, January 4-11, 1997, pp. 39-45.

Ramesh, P. and Trivedi, M.L., "Role of Organizational Efficiency in Improving Productivity: A Macro-Level Evidence from Indian Industry", *Artha Vijnana*, Vol. XXXVII, No. 2, June 1995, pp. 129-137.

Rao, A. and Sita, C., "Human Resource Management Practices in India: An Explanatory Study", *Indian Journal of Industrial Relations*, Vol. 30, No. 2, October 1994, pp. 190-202.

Rao, Hanumantha, C.H., "Economic Reforms, Agricultural Growth and Rural Poverty", *Indian Economic Journal*, Vol. 43, No. 4, April-June, 1995-96, pp. 1-12.

Rao, Hanumantha, K., "Conduit-Indian Social and Economic Development: Index to the Literature" (Book Review), *Journal of Rural Development*, Vol. 14, No. 4, October-December, 1995, pp. 460-462.

Rao, S.L., "Rural Development and Service Delivery", *The Economic Times*, December 11, 1995, p. 6.

Ravallion, M., "Policy Forum: Poverty and Development-Issue in Measuring and Modelling Poverty", *The Economic Journal*, Vol. 106, No. 438, September 1996, pp. 1326-1328.

Ray, Manushi, "Economics of Population and Development", *Economic and Political Weekly*, Vol. XXX, No. 36, September 9, 1995, pp. 2263-2266.

Sathyanala, C., "Reproductive Health Consequences of Bhopal Gas Leak: Fertility and Gynaecological Disorders", *Economic and Political Weekly*, Vol. XXXI, January 6, 1996, pp. 43-57.

Sattinger, Michael, "General Equilibrium Effects of Unemployment Compensation with Labourforce Participation", *Journal of Labour Economics*, Vol. 13, No. 4, October 1995, pp. 623-652.

Shankar, Kripa, "Sorry State of U.P.'s Economy", *Economic and Political Weekly*, Vol. XXX, No. 12, March 25, 1995, pp. 609-610.

Shariff, Abusaleh, "Socio-Economic and Demographic Differences Between Hindu and Muslims in India", *Economic and Political Weekly*, Vol. XXX, No. 46, November 1995, pp. 2947-2952.

Sharma, B.B.L., "When Health Care is Not Free", *The Economic Times*, February 17, 1996, p. 5.

Sharma, Vijay, Pal, Gajja, B.L. and Shah, D., "Managing Land and Water Resources for Sustainable Agricultural Development: Issues and Options", *Artha Vijnana*, Vol. XXXVII, No. 1, March 1995, pp. 46-65.

Shergill, H.S. and Singh, Gurmail, "Poverty in Rural Punjab: Trend over Green Revolution Decades", *Economic and Political Weekly*, Vol. XXX, No. 25, June 24, 1995, pp. A.80-83.

Shields, Michael, P., "Time Ledonic Migration and Household Production", *Journal of Regional Science,* Vol. 35, No. 1, February 1995, pp. 117-134.

Shiva, Vandana, "Agricultural Biodiversity, Intellectual Property Rights and Farmers' Rights", *Economic and Political Weekly*, Vol. XXXI, No. 25, June 22, 1996, pp. 1621-1623.

Shivamaggi, H.B., "Rural Credit: New Role of AFC", *Economic and Political Weekly*, Vol. XXXI, Nos.41&42, October 12-19, 1996, pp. 2791-2792.

Shripathi, K.P., "Performance of Rural Development Projects by Voluntary Agencies", *Journal of Rural Development"*, Vol. 14, No. 4, October-December 1995, pp. 431-442.

Shrivastava, M.M.P., "Sustainable Development with Special Reference to Environment and Agriculture", *Journal of Rural Development*, Vol. 13, No. 1, January-March, 1994, pp. 47-56.

Shylendra, H.S., "Farm Loan Waivers: A Distributional and Impact Analysis of the Agricultural and Rural Debt Relief Scheme, 1990", *Artha Vijnana*, Vol. XXXVII, No. 3, September 1995, pp. 261-275.

Siegel, Paul, B., Alwang, Jeffrey and Johnson, Thomas, G., "A Structural Decomposition of Regional Economic Instability: A Conceptual Framework", *Journal of Regional Science*, Vol. 35, No. 3, 1995, pp. 457-470.

Singh, Amrik, "The Place of Secondary Education", *Economic and Political Weekly*, Vol. XXXII, No. 17, April 26-May 2, 1997, pp. 880-883.

Singh, Joginder and Banerjee, Ashok, "Agricultural Situation on Eve of Monsoon", *Economic and Political Weekly*, Vol. XXX, No. 28, July 15, 1995, pp. 1732-1733.

Singh, Man Mohan, "New Economic Policy and Challenges Before the Labour Economics", *Indian Journal of Labour Economics*, Vol. 36, No. 1, January-March, 1993, pp. 3-7.

Singh, P.K., Singh, Jaspal, Mahnot, S.C. and Modi, Sanjay, "Watershed Approach in Improving the Socio-Economic Status of Tribal Area: A Case Study" *Journal of Rural Development*, Vol14, No. 2, April-June, 1995, pp. 107-116.

Singh, Sukhpal, "Relative Economic Efficiency of Indian Rural Producers' Cooperatives: A Review of Evidence and Research Issues", *Journal of Rural Development*, Vol. 13, No. 1, January-March, 1994, pp. 115-128.

Singh, Sukhpal, "Structural Adjustment Programme and Indian Agriculture", *Economic and Political Weekly*, Vol. XXX, No. 51, December 23, 1995, pp. 3311-3314.

Singh, Tarlok, "Money Prices Causality in India: An Empirical Investigation", *Indian Journal of Economics*, Vol. LXXV, Part III, No. 299, 1995, pp. 447-478.

Sjodhka, Surinder, "Beyond the Economics of Supply and Demand", *Economic and Political Weekly*, Vol. XXXI, No. 47, November 23, 1996, pp. 3057-3058.

Slesnick, D.T., "Consumption and Poverty: How Effective are Im-kind Transfers?", *The Economic Journal*, Vol. 106, No. 439, November 1996, pp. 1527-1545.

Souza, Errol, D., "Economic Reforms: Ringside View",

Index

L

M

N

P

Q

R

S